Five Great Healers Speak Here

Cover art by *Jane A Evans*

Five Great Healers Speak Here

Compiled by
Nancy and Esmond Gardner

*This publication made possible with
the assistance of the Kern Foundation*

The Theosophical Publishing House
Wheaton, IL U.S.A.
Madras, India / London, England

Library of Congress Cataloging in Publication Data
Five great healers speak here.

   "A Quest book."
   Includes bibliographical references.
   1. Spiritual healing and spiritualism—Addresses,
essays, lectures. 2. Mental healing—Addresses, essays,
lectures. 3. Healers—Biography. I. Gardner, Nancy,
1909-   . II. Gardner, Esmond, 1901-   .
BF1275.F3F58   1982   615.8'52   82-50164
ISBN 0-8356-0567-1 (pbk.)

Printed in the United States of America

Miracle: A marvelous event occurring within human experience which cannot have been brought about by human power or by the operation of any natural agency, and must therefore be ascribed to the special intervention of the Deity or of some supernatural being; chiefly an act (e.g. of healing) exhibiting control over the laws of nature, and serving as evidence that the agent is either divine or is specially favored by God.

The Oxford English Dictionary
1961 reprinted edition

Contents

There is a principle which is a bar against all information, which is proof against all arguments and which cannot fail to keep a man in everlasting ignorance . . . that principle is contempt prior to investigation.

Herbert Spencer

> In this mental universe
> I have a body
> but I *am* a soul
> and its thoughts
> are living things.

PREFACE

Swift as the crack of lightning or slow and steady as the compulsion of the tide, mysterious healings through human channels have occurred repeatedly. Throughout human history, some people with a compelling drive of compassion have been healing their fellow men with the force of their minds. They use spoken suggestions in hypnotic treatment, magnetic touch, invocations to a higher power, or any individual method that works for them. The reported cases of spirit and magnetic healing cover every type of disability.

While attending a seminar on the occult arts in Switzerland, we came upon the idea of compiling a book on such healing. Psychics, healers, mediums, astrologers and practitioners of all the related arts were gathered to instruct us. When the excitement of the seminar had died down and we sorted out our feelings about it, we were left with a deep impression of the beauty and worthwhile service of the healers gathered there. They had struck a chord in our hearts that continued to vibrate. We realized vividly that healing is an act of compassion and of great service to others.

We found that most gifted healers hold one belief in common, that they serve only as a channel, an instrument or conductor. The healing power comes from a higher source. We began to wonder if this mystical gift is exclusive to some rare individuals, or is it an inborn faculty available to us all — one that can be used constantly like sight, voice and hearing.

The thought occurred to us that an identical set of

questions might be asked of a few of the great healers of proven talent, in order to find out where they agree in their methods and thinking or how their ideas differ. By this process a common denominator or foundation could be found. We also wanted to discover whether the art of healing could be learned.

We mentioned the concept to some healers who were enthusiastic about the project and eager to be of help to all who aspire to develop their healing powers in the service of others. The questions and subquestions were then developed in detail in an effort to cover the subject fully. The replies of the five healers seemed to us important and illuminating.

This project opened the way for us to get better acquainted with our healers. We will share our impressions of these unusual and dedicated people in the chapters that follow, along with biographical sketches of them, preceding their own words.

As these five great healing channels speak to us on the pages of this book, their thoughts and individual techniques should bring us closer to an understanding of how their powers are exercised, and perhaps answer the question: Can miraculous healing be learned by any dedicated student? The power to heal may turn out to be a higher energy which we can all use but fail to actualize because of doubt and neglect. Encouraged by the wisdom of these five healers and the reality of their experience, we may discover and practice using the healing energy, and find it is our birthright. The compassionate effort in itself will strengthen the giver and in time—the receiver.

Nancy and Esmond Gardner

INTRODUCTION

Dolores Krieger, Ph.D., R.N.

Healing is one of the most humane of human acts. Historically, the ability to heal has been regarded in most cultures as a Divine gift from God, the bestower of life, to a few who were dedicated to a holy way, and in the past the role of healer and priest were one. Today, however, one of the signs of our times is an unprecedented proliferation of modes of healing and an unexpected significant increase in the number of persons who want to learn to heal. However, most of these modalities are oriented towards self-healing and most of the people learning them do so from a deep-seated need to become personally healed, or whole (from the Middle English derivative of the verb to heal: *haelen*, to make whole), for this is an age marked by a pandemic of stress-related illnesses that spin off from the daily uncertainties of contemporary existence on our planet.

The book we have before us, however, is concerned with persons who play the role of healer not for their own healing but for the healing of others. Yet paradoxically most persons who play the role of healer will readily agree to two acknowledgements: that the first person they heal is, indeed, themselves, and that in the final analysis one must admit that it is the healee, the patient, who heals her/himself. One might say that the healer acts as a human support system which therapeutically bolsters the ill person's depleted energy, energy that is called by various names in different cultures. To the Chinese it is the *ch'i*, to the Egyptian it is known as the *ka*, in Sanskrit it is called *prana*, in Tibetan *ylur*, and among the Hawaiian Kahuna its name is *mana*. Whatever the culture, however, the healer goes through a personalized ritual, an individualized experience in interiorization in order to heal. In this book we have five such accounts from healers of extensive experience.

In reviewing the literature on healing, one is impressed that although healing per se is not restricted to one belief system, nevertheless, there is a general concurrence of opinion among healers, even though they may come from the most disparate of cultures, on how the healing of human beings occurs. LeShan made a survey of the literature in order to seek out " . . . explanations or theories of explanations" and found that they could be categorized into three general classes:

1. The largest number of healers described their work as "prayer," and they considered their success to be due to the direct intervention of God.

2. A second group was quite certain that the healings were done by "spirits," that the person who was playing the role of healer in some manner had created a "special" linkage between these spirits and the healee.

3. A third group believed that they were transmitters, channels or originators of a unique type of energy which had healing effects.[1]

Dr. LeShan was concerned with the question of the relationship of the paranormal to the world of everyday reality. What the present book explores through the experiences of five well-known healers is this question (paraphrasing LeShan): What is the relationship between the healer and the rest of reality at the moment of the healing enactment? From this brief collation of the philosophies of five healers, each with a significantly different cultural background and healing mode, we can see that a valid argument can be developed for a consistency of experience between these healers and their universe at the moment of the healing enactment. In summary, the major points of agreement are:

1. The primary source of healing is Divinity, called by whatever name, and the energetics of the healing enactments are aroused by compassion, which stimulates self-regeneration in the patient.

2. Healing is a natural concommitant of a personal relationship with spirit or one's higher self.

3. Help can come from other than living, human sources, i.e., Guides, Water Spirits, Tree Brothers and being with flowers.

4. Karma at one and the same time provides both limitation and access to the healing process. A clue to the access is via the patient coming into relationship with her/his higher self, and in this the healer can act as teacher or facilitator.

5. The importance of faith, acceptance and surrender on the part of the patient, but nevertheless even skeptics can be healed.

6. Healing is not a special gift for the few but is a practice that can be learned by persons who are willing to devote themselves to the learning process.

A few examples will serve to illustrate these points.

THE PRIMARY HEALING SOURCE

The primary source of the healing is compassion, says Gurudev Chitrabhanu, one of the leading Jain masters. Healing occurs through the act of blessing the healee (patient), blessings which he sees as an energy source. To heal, however, it is necessary to "walk in unity with God." Brother Mandus, founder of the World Healing Crusades, also sees the primary source of healing as based on compassion, but this compassion is conceived by him as welling up from the combined efforts of "praying partners" who are " . . . focused upon the physical perfection shining in the patient." He feels that the underlying principle of healing is that " . . . the body has a natural regeneration which is a built-in intelligence."

This statement clearly agrees with the world-renowned English healer, Harry Edwards, whose conclusion after a lifetime of healing is that the basis of healing lies in " . . . the natural healing intelligences of the body." He, too, says that the source of spiritual healing is God, and that the intelligent direction of a healing force originates from a spiritual realm which is, he says, " . . . a common heritage of the human family."

"All power is from above," says Oh Shinnah, whose experience is grounded equally in the ancient traditions of the Amerindians and modern research and teaching. She sees power as being "expressions (of the) path to the Source of all . . . . We channel the powers of healing through an opening made by our love, compassion and surrender."

For Mama Mona, President of the African Spiritual Church in South Africa, the primary source of all healing is God. She speaks of the importance of " . . . the full power of prayer," and sees singing as a mode of attunement which "raises the power." To the question of how her healing works she responds quite simply and quite elegantly: " . . . some of the things I do are as mysterious to me as to you." However, she does state that the radiation of love is fundamental to healing.

ATTUNEMENT WITH HIGHER SELF

Chitrabhanu feels that prayer is one mode of communication with the higher self and that through it both patient and healer "can learn to function on that higher dimension." The importance of being on center, of finding that sense of quietude within, is that it is the equivalent of being "in the company of the eternal." Chitrabhanu clearly says that the healer should be in unity with the healing force and attune to one's higher self, for then a deep love, compassion and mental balance flow freely. In so doing, the healer shows the patient how to heal her/himself.

Brother Mandus sees the healer as a "praying partner," an intercessor, who is caught up and illumined by God as a channel through which " . . . the infinite perfection of God shines."

Oh Shinnah emphasizes that by " . . . becoming free of the attachment to being the doer," one thereby becomes " . . . an integral part of the doing," the healing process itself. "Anyone who wishes to help 'make better' must develop a deep sense of love and compassion, which is a reflection of one's spiritual self." She continues, "Healing is innate . . . . Life (itself) is the gift of touch. We serve, and that is all we do." She speaks strongly to the importance of developing a true sense of commitment to be disciplined in all modes of healing, and to the necessity of " . . . the practice of surrender in the every-day events of our lives." Vivid word pictures bring to life the moment of her insight into the healing enactment: "Illuminated, the spark of my essence caught fire . . . consuming rage and regret."

OTHER THAN HUMAN AGENTS OF HEALING

Brother Mandus agrees in the potential of human resources when he says: "Healing is everyone's ability and facility." In addition, Brother Mandus has no difficulty in perceiving that help in the healing act can come from other than human resources: " . . . there could be a Heavenly Host helping with Divine Healing Services. I have no difficulty in believing that shining ones in the next plane of vibration, or even loved ones, can come into the atmosphere of prayer to help someone on Earth in the healing scene."

Oh Shinnah confirms that healing does not only come

through the " . . . two-leggeds. The Water Spirits and the Tree Brothers require only that one be in need of healing and approach them . . . . The healer couples energies with the forces of nature and spirit." She tells of a very tall Indian man, Mithra, who consistently came to her when she was ill as a child. "To me it has always been natural to call upon the spirits for various reasons," she says. "No one ever told me it was special or different."

This presence is perceived by Edwards in the form of spirit Guides. He states: "It is not the healer who administers the healing treatment, but the healing intelligence or Guide. The healer himself does not heal." However, he clearly states that the healer should " . . . cooperate intelligently with the healing process which is based on . . . law-governed healing forces that induce change." The healer accepts the flow of thought without question, and is receptive to intuition, but keeps the information in reserve until there is "substantial" proof.

Mama Mona also listens to spirit Guides: "Guidance comes in messages when I tend my flowers." These messages are "precise and clear." Color is of great importance in Mama Mona's healing, as is timing.

THE PLACE OF KARMA

Within the context of Mama Mona's cultural heritage, reincarnation is an accepted basic assumption. Such a belief logically includes a concept of karma, and it is possibly because of this frame of reference that healing is thought to occur when the next of kin, who can be looked upon as the living representatives of one's inherited consequences of past lives, comes and creates the power to heal the one who is ill. This is done through a ritual cleansing before seeking the ancestor's forgiveness on behalf of the sick.

Chitrabhanu, too, sees the centrality of the individual's karma to healing. "Healing," he says, "is the burning of karma." Only insofar as an individual's karma permits, however, will a healing take place. It is important for the healer to know the Self so that one can intelligently deal with the question of karma, the present consequences of past-life experiences.

Oh Shinnah also perceives that in certain cases illness may be a reflection of past-life experience. "We treat the entire family," she points out, "believing that the most sensitive and vulnerable reflect the whole." Each healing is designed for the total problem including mind, body, soul and spirit.

THE PATIENT'S ATTITUDE

Chitrabhanu points to the importance of the patient recognizing Self and identifying with the Self. In discussing the reduction of symptoms, he also speaks to the importance of anticipation, conviction and faith that healing will take place. However, if karma is too heavy (or "sticky") for healing to take place, an enlightened teacher can show the patient how to "bear it with peace and balance."

Brother Mandus also sees the importance of faith, stating that there is a direct relation between the stature of a healer and the degree of belief and acceptance in the patient. A sense of inadequacy, "this uncertainty factor," must be swept aside, he says.

Edwards perceives the issue somewhat differently, acknowledging that a strong desire to be well can naturally accelerate healing. However, he believes that regardless of conscious cooperation, the patient's spirit acts as a transformer and is able to receive healing forces through the spirit self. He states flatly: "Spiritual healing is superior to all of man's ideas."

Oh Shinnah states it in these terms: "The skeptic
. . . will be affected by the healing vibrations . . .
because . . . the true transforming power is
love." She explains: "When one is led to the path of a
healer, a self-healing begins and, through this realization,
one finds union with Source. One walks the path to power
when we find our spiritual selves; the world of spirit
becomes accessible."

LEARNING TO HEAL

All the healers agree that healing is not a special gift
limited to a few but can be learned. Brother Mandus
points out that healing takes place in all ministries,
regardless of persuasion, and that there is no one
exclusive pattern which it follows. He says: "It would
almost seem that the moment anyone opens an aperture
of love, faith, prayer, or awareness of something beyond
human power, then the spirit floodlights through the
aperture to help and bless, irrespective and regardless of
the definition of the healer, the method, or the technique."

Harry Edwards feels would-be healers first must have
certain character traits: generosity, sympathy, compassion, a desire to be of service. In addition, they must
"inwardly feel they have an insistent desire to be able to
take away pain and unhappiness . . . . This desire to
heal must come from the heart." Then "they may well
possess the latent powers of spirit healing," which he feels
takes time to develop.

Mama Mona acknowledges that there are many healers
among Africans: "It seems that this gift is common among
the African people." One's psychic powers can be
improved by dedication and use, according to her. "Ask
and ye shall be given, look and it shall be open to you."

Oh Shinnah, too, feels most of us could be healers if we
are dedicated, but that society is not conducive to this.

"Healing is innate within most of our natures," she tells us. However, it does not blossom without effort on our part. "Anyone who wishes to enhance the world through healing must become a dedicated student of light within and without themselves." Thus she encourages us to pursue our inherent abilities.

However, Chitrabhanu warns us against using the ability to heal to bolster our self-importance or accentuate our separated selves, which can block healing. "No person should claim that he or she is a healer," he tells us. "That is one of the things that creates a kind of duality in the mind of the healer himself, a dependence on his own powers . . . there must be a unity with the healing force, no ego-separation."

THE MYSTICAL WORLD-VIEW

These examples of the healers' views on various points indicate a powerful body of agreement. However, upon deep analysis, it can be seen that the difference in background of these healers is neither the significant variable nor the essential reality. What is of decisive importance is that all of their perceptions are embedded in a mystical perspective.

The religious literature describes five direct ways in which Spirit makes an impact on human beings: experience with angels and demons, through dreams and visions, in prophecy, through the medium of special divine knowledge and wisdom, and through the healing enactment. All these personal knowledges are in the domain of the mystical. These experiences based on direct perception are diametrically opposed to the hard-core scientific stance which relies on mechanistic models which specifically exclude consideration of consciousness, spirit or any factor other than objective data about the external world and cause-effect explanation. In contrast, the way of the mystic has been termed "an excursion into an inner world" to which one has direct entree, and therefore personal knowledge, of the implicate or enfolded order of the universe. The literature tells of the many mystics of the past who have been in direct communication with spirit guides or disincarnate teachers, mystics such as Plotinus, Meister Eckhart, St. Theresa of Avila, Emmanuel Swedenborg, Ramakrishna and others of similar repute. Krippner and Villoldo, in looking at the lives of mystics such as these, note that they all report a unique world view in which they perceive a fundamental unity among all things, the recognition of an illusory nature to such man-made constructs as time, space, etc., and the importance of acquiring information other than through the accepted five senses.[2]

LeShan agrees with this. He calls this the realm of the transpsychic reality. In reference to healing he says:

> Instead of using will and determination to try to bend the cosmic energies to your purpose, you try to become attuned to these energies so that you become a clear channel for them. It means a complete surrender of your own will except for your desire for the best for the healee. Here you identify with the All totally, and reach toward the state where you wear the universe like a glove and it wears you.[3]

That is, one changes and is thereby changed by the "cosmic energies." This numinous realm has been conceived as a non-material background or field which provides the fundamental basis of material existence, from which our familiar world arises.[4] In this world-view, sometimes called theosophy, the human being is seen as caught in and absorbed by the material processes of life, without realizing that these processes are in actuality transient and illusory. For as one examines the organization and intrinsic order of the processes of nature and in man, it becomes apparent that their patterning or relationships are determined by the underlying reality of non-material domains analogous to our concept of physical force fields. Thus the seemingly "real" world of ordinary experience is an outworking of the non-material "cosmic energies" or fields. This view is highly significant in relation to healing, for paradoxically, human interaction can serve to "change" or influence the fields. To be effective this requires a deeply conscious act stemming from self-direction and self-awareness, both characteristics of the higher self which is rooted in this same background field (called Atman in Eastern terminology).

It is from this highest, unitive level that true healing derives. Consonant with universal laws of hierarchy or levels of organization, if one "works" (for example, heals someone) at the highest/deepest levels of the human condition (at the level of the higher Self), then in effect one is working at all levels at once. Therefore, if one can center and reach an inner state of quietude characteristic of that level, even for a moment, that alignment or equipoise of energies that are in fact one's Self can have an enormous effect to the good on self and on others.[5] This is the act we know as the healing interaction, an enactment of the fullness of the human stature. We look to books such as the one before us, books concerning those who heal, in order to better understand its profound complexities.

REFERENCES

1. Lawrence LeShan. *The Medium, the Mystic and the Physicist*. New York: Ballantine Books, 1976, pp. 102-103.

2. Stanley Krippner and Alberto Villoldo. *The Realms of Healing*. Millbrae: Celestial Arts, 1976, p. 176.

3. LeShan, *op. cit.*, p. 151.

4. F.L. Kunz. *The Quest for the Quiet Mind*. Wheaton: The Theosophical Publishing House, 1956.

5. Dora Kunz. Second Pumpkin Hollow Farm Invitational Healers' Conference, Craryville, New York, 1973.

*Gurudev Shree
Chitrabhanu*

BIOGRAPHICAL SKETCH

Munishree Chitrabhanu, a profound and brilliant teacher, is one of the spiritual leaders of India's 4,000,000 Jains, a religion little known outside India. Yoga and Jainism share the principles of non-violence. Munishree has stated: "There is nothing in the world so powerful as non-violence."

He explains that the Jain philosophy is not essentially founded on any particular writing or external revelation but on the unfolding of spiritual consciousness, which is the birthright of every soul. Through knowledge and endeavor, the individual develops and unfolds the potential within him.

Munishree defines a Jain as a man who speaks of personal responsibility for his own deeds, regards a person as master of his own destiny, and refrains from violence. Whether he calls himself a Jain or not is unimportant. "I look for a change of soul, not a label."

Munishree is broadly ecumenical in his approach to spirituality. He says, "I do not want to teach people their duties or any doctrines of religion. I want to arouse them from their complacencies, to stir their hearts, to vivify their imaginations, to bring them to the heights of which they are capable." He describes a true religious leader as the small boat which takes the spiritual pilgrim from the shore to the deep-water vessel of spirituality out in the harbor.

Born in a village in Rajputana to a middle-class family on July 26th, 1922, Roop Rajendra (as he was named) attended college at Bangalore. At the age of sixteen he experienced a spiritual awakening which led him to make a pilgrimage to the holy shrines of India.

When he took the vows of a monk, he promised to "protect all life, speak the truth and to take with a joyful heart what is given." As a Jain Saddu (monk) he traveled on foot more than 30,000 miles and for a period of five years spoke to no one except his master. Although Munishree renounced the material world at the age of twenty, he is no ascetic but an enlightened man of action.

In 1964, he succeeded to the leadership of the Jain religion and also became the founder of the Divine Knowledge Society in Bombay, which operates medical centers and food stations throughout India and strives to improve the status of women.

Munishree is the first Jain Master to come to the West. When he decided to leave India in order to help build the bridge from East to West, he generated controversy by breaking the ancient ban on monks traveling by vehicle. Some of the more orthodox members of the Jain community protested. But Munishree pointed out that traveling by jet did not involve cruelty to animals, the original reason for the prohibition. "Some rules and conventions," he said, "were created to meet the need of their times and some are no longer applicable. The law of life is change; man must change with the times or perish. Unfortunately, people do not have the courage to confront outdated theologies, customs and institutions. Out of a false sense of security, they reject change."

Munishree also broke Jain monastic tradition by his marriage to Promoda Shah. They now have two sons born in the United States.

Munishree arrived in America as one of two representatives of Indian spiritual culture invited to address the Third Spiritual Summit Conference held at Harvard Divinity School. Now residing in New York City, Munishree has taught at the State University of New

York, the New School, and lectured at universities such as Princeton and Cornell as well as many preparatory schools and churches. He has formed an organization called New Life Now which is dedicated to helping him bring his spiritual doctrine to this part of the world.

"To feel at home on this earth in these tremendous times," Munishree says, "we need the state of consciousness in which we can experience harmony with ourselves and with the universe. Only then can man build a just and peaceful society. Be it a country or a race, individual or community, its decline irrevocably sets in from the moment it succumbs to an insular view or an intolerance of other peoples views."

According to Munishree, the role of the spiritual leader in the New Age is to guide society away from useless conventions and artificial barriers to what precisely is the purpose of life. "A reformer," he says, "must make bold moves at times. Otherwise he cannot achieve his aims and strengthen his cause."

Munishree's teachings are direct, clear and full of images. He is the author of twenty-six books and several volumes of poetry. Many of his books are translated into English. He is an authority on comparative religion, a master of Sanskrit.

As a spiritual guide, he discourages his students from following him for more than two years. "By that time," he claims, "the devotee should be strong enough in body, mind, and soul to take charge of his own spiritual journey. A Guru must never foster dependence in his disciples."

Munishree teaches meditation as an integral part of daily life, not as an escape from reality. "Meditation," he says, "teaches us to look at the still, deep, inner recesses of our souls. This leads to self-knowledge and ultimately to the point where the inner voice will speak to the seeker."

Since Munishree Chitrabhanu lives in Manhattan when

he is not in India, we were able to attend many of his seminars and informal gatherings. Muni's face and eyes are alight with kindness, inspiration and the bravery of original thought, for Muni is a philosopher as well as a healer of the body and spirit. We stretched our minds to absorb his vivid words and his way of describing the inner spiritual journey by relating small fables that sink into the subconscious and rise from time to time to nudge the conscious mind.

Sprinkled here and there in his talks are original suggestions. For example, he recommends placing oneself a little to one side of one's body in thought and saying to it as to a friend, "How are you?" If the mind wanders when one is trying to meditate, he suggests asking of it, "Where have you been?" When being taught spiritual illumination by an inspired teacher, Muni advises that we mentally reach out a hand toward that light and say simply, "Let me have it." Clearly Muni is unique.

He warns us against living for pleasure. "Those who live mainly for pleasure die quite soon, if not physically, then their portion of wisdom expires. This is because they are *consumers* of energy. But those who *give* energy receive it."

While attending one of his informal sessions, someone asked Muni if he had any hobbies. "Of course," said Muni. "I am a collector. Where other people collect stamps or objects of art, I collect blessings. Other collections remain here but my hoard of blessings can be transformed into pure energy and I can take it with me when I go. When you help someone and that person speaks from the heart, 'God bless, live long,' that is a collectable blessing."

Munishree Chitrabhanu is an unfailing beacon to all who come within his force field. His warmth and wisdom have gained him the love of people from all walks of life. He is an ambassador of harmony as he affirms the oneness of all life.

CHITRABHANU SPEAKS

The primary source of the healing power is compassion. You must be concerned with loving a fellow being. When you bring to this charity, serenity of heart, and balance of mind, you are on your way to becoming a channel for healing. A feeling of sharing and caring flows out and from that flow comes healing. I call that force a blessing rather than healing. To call it healing limits it. And it may not always work. But a blessing has no interest other than to bless and to benefit, and this is a pure energy, overall energy.

Christ did not come into the world as a demonstrator, saying, I am a healer, watch me heal. He blessed people and the pure vibration of compassion within him connected with God's healing laws. Thus, people were healed. He was a spiritual person living in a dimension of love and compassion and, thereby, worked miracles.

Why is a human channel necessary for healing?

In most cases because the concept of God varies among people. God is not a person but a high, pure energy. If you can understand God only as being a person, then the problem of petition arises and the currying of favor. Some of us personify the God energy as a person sitting in a chair and governing the world, an old grandfather or a potentate hungry for praise who may respond to our petition by saying, "What do you want, my child?"

If that is your level, step higher. Our minds cannot exist without projecting something or forming something. It is vital to do this correctly and to understand that in order to reach the high, pure vibration of the light of

7

God, we must learn to raise ourselves beyond our present level.

Know that everything is in abundance in the universe and you walk in unity with God who will, if you communicate as you would with a beloved, wise companion, give you spirtual light and guidance. This joy and benefit can only be achieved by going within yourself to the center.

That is why the real teachers have said that the heaven we seek is not outside, or in the blue of the sky, but within. So, ultimately we must find our path, learn the way ot our own center instead of looking up. If we want to learn to dispense blessings to others, we must realize that they can come only from the richness of our kingdom within.

What is the difference between magnetic, spiritual, and faith healing?

When you receive outer help, such as hypnosis or human energy through the hands, then it can be called magnetic healing. When someone helps you to contact your powers within, it is called a spiritual healing. To illustrate faith healing, the monks in our monasteries bless people by sprinkling them with a compound of saffron and camphor and send their compassionate prayers and good thoughts with it. The powder is called vasaxet. It means "dispensing the fragrance." They do not attempt a healing at that time. Suppose the people are not healed; then they blame the fathers, saying, "Our teacher blessed us with this powder and we are not healed." So they lose faith in it and thus deprive themselves of some valuable communication with the blessing directed at them. Faith often completes the circuit of energy and light.

Can anyone be a healer?

There are many healers who use various techniques, gestures, words and demonstrations, all designed to make the patient feel that something is being done for him. In general the patient is not too highly evolved or enlightened. Therefore he cannot read the mind of the would-be healer. He believes that all those demonstrations mean that something is being done for him. A healer may hold his hand up skyward and say, "I am bringing down energy," and the patient will think, "Oh, My God, how much energy he is drawing down to me." But if the healer sits calmly and sends beautiful vibrations, the patient will think indignantly, "He is not doing anything —he is just sitting there relaxing!"

Many healers make significant gestures and appear to summon great powers in order to convince and help the patient. Conviction is the main thing. So many illnesses have started from doubt, fear, and ignorance of natural laws. But with absolute faith, these fears are removed and the person is again in a state of health, perhaps temporary for most hypnotism anesthetizes the pain or sickness and lasts only a few weeks.

A capable healer can treat any person and deal with any disease, and for ten days the person will not feel any pain if a deep impression has been made on his subconscious mind. This must be created in part before the patient arrives. He should be told that the healer has tremendous power to heal. One touch and he will feel marvelous, his disease will be gone. Before the sick person comes into the presence, he anticipates. When he meets the healer, he feels the aura that has been built up. Soon he feels convinced that he is completely cured of his condition. The matter is there, but his mind has worked on it, so his disorder has subsided. But the patient has not really been cured of the cause of his disease, although the symptoms have relaxed. The inner conviction that the person is healed will fade with time and the pressure of the outside world.

No person should claim that he or she is a healer. That

is one of the things that creates a kind of duality in the mind of the healer himself, a dependence on his own powers. In the physical world it is a fact that some are doctors and some are not. But, in the spiritual world, there must be unity with the healing force, no ego separation. You must raise yourself (the simplicity of your education is of no importance) to a state of purity of love, of compassion, and mental balance, so that your healing or blessing emanates from a pure and holy master. At that level, the blessing works powerfully and smoothly because the healer himself does not get in the way of the healing force.

For example, there was a holy man in India who was so pure a soul that people came from all over to collect his blessings, which had great healing power. One day it came to the holy man's mind that this was not good because he was seeing their faces and saying to himself, "This man came to me for a blessing from a great distance," or, "This girl is desperate for my blessing." It all seemed a pitfall for his ego.

Therefore, he made a decision. He would give his blessings only to those who waited behind him, out of sight. He would give no more blessings to the persons who came in front of him and whom he could see. If they were not visible to him and asked for a complete blessing, he would say, "Go your way, you are blessed."

The holy man wanted to see only the spiritual and to be equal to the people he was helping. He wanted no part of such thinking as, "I am in a position to help you and you are in a position to receive my help." Such superiority is putting one person down and another up, and it was not for him. The holy man knew that you can climb the highest spiritual mountain, and when you reach the summit, who is waiting to shake hands with you but your ego!

Both sage and saint realize that power is dangerous if

one feels, "You are in need and I can supply it." So, on the highest level, the person does not want to make anybody feel that he is obligated by received blessings; no obligation should be felt. The blessing benefits both giver and receiver.

Does the healer project an invisible healing light?

When the healer or the saint or the person who has been consulted reaches for attunement with his higher self and achieves it, he feels a flow of brilliant light flooding him. He truly sees the person who has come to him and prays; "Oh let me, let me send my blessings, let me send light from this brilliance I experience." Then love and compassion flow from him.

Is the healer tired or refreshed after a treatment?

Why? It is not any physical exercise or an athletic process. However, you may get tired if you use fantastic gestures to denote drawing energy as if you were pulling a kite down. But in the spiritual process, the healer or saint is in tune. He becomes a pool of energy and blessings and the pool becomes full and overflows in a river of light. If you are full of light, what can possibly come in to tire or disturb you?

Does the healer connect with a healing guide?

Our guide is within our own spirit or soul. But the qualities needed there must be cultivated. One quality is knowledge, another is vision, a third is bliss, and the fourth infinite power. Each soul has the possibility of these four qualities, so he does not have to connect with any guide. He needs no outside power. The four qualities are our own natural endowment.

If the connection is difficult, the healer must sit quietly and meditate upon those who have achieved these four characteristics fully. We call this "sitavan" which means, "I bow to all the perfect souls." In this way the healer becomes humble as he bows to all the souls who have achieved these four qualities in completeness. He can raise his consciousness to the level of Sita and there receive the energy of the great ones.

What is the healer's procedure?

I do not consider myself other than a monk and a philosopher. I specialize in showing the patient how to heal himself. I suggest that, in his imagination, he stand slightly away from his body and throw the light of his consciousness on the problem. His attitude can be light-hearted and playful, saying to himself, perhaps, "How are you?" Feeling detached and relaxed, he can then go about projecting the healing energy himself, imagining that he is appealing to the healing intelligence of his cells to repair the body wherever necessary. Actually he is using a powerful force, the truth of the imagination.

Are there any limitations on the healing process?

The limitations are karma. Karma is an all-important factor in a healing or a blessing. If the karma is heavy, the efforts of the healer cannot succeed. Karma is the sum to date of your past actions in this life and in your previous lifetimes. It is the reaction and boomerang return of your deeds and thoughts and is constantly being modified by your present actions and thoughts. It is an absolute law, as forceful as an invisible wind that bends us with its power like so many trees, uprooting some and, when we die, blowing our souls into new situations like so many seeds.

Some children are born into luxury and some in ghettos. Some mothers worry because their babies will not drink enough milk; others worry because they cannot buy enough milk. These wide differences are due to their karmas. They have taken their places in the world according to the immutable law of Karma.

The working out of karma is sometimes compared to four people playing cards. Each is dealt thirteen different cards which correspond to the karma they have accumulated. It can happen that those with good hands make no effort to play well, feeling secure in their good fortune, while the indifferent or poor hands can be played brilliantly and sometimes win all the points.

If you are unhappy in your present life, you may have inflicted misery on someone in a previous life. That suffering will return to you. It circles and comes back in the eternal law of action and reaction. If we perform right actions, we will build good karma.

If we are ready to be healed and enlightened, we will fall from the tree like ripe fruit when the blessing and healing power is felt. But if we are not ready, if our Karma is heavy, we will not leave the tree no matter how forceful a shake the human energy brought to heal us can give the bough. We will remain there, and the blessing and compassion do not change our condition.

No healer can take complete responsibility on his head and say, "I am going to heal you." That disturbs the law of the universe, which is not governed by one healer or one person. If he claims that he is able to heal any kind of disease, that is ignorance of the law, or he is on an ego trip, setting himself above the laws of the universe.

However, instead of saying to sick people as so many do who accept the law of reincarnation, "It is your fate, you have earned it, endure it," the healer should point the way out of this condition. With the present disorder of the body, he should point out that it is important to keep a strong spiritual level. When we are negative, we are below our level and then illness comes. We have gone out of nature, out of balance, and we have not lived a life in tune with the natural laws of love, compassion, and humanity. We must know constantly that our thoughts are living things with vibrations that can bless or harm us. Send out only thoughts that will come back to you with high vibrations bearing interest. Interest is the extra compassion we give.

The healer should explain that karma can be

understood in terms of weaving. By your behavior, you sow the seed, spin the cotton to make the thread, and weave the cloth that you must wear in the future. The garment can lie on you like a heavy rug that no healing or blessing can lift, for it would be going against the laws of the universe.

During your life time, your karma can be recorded in four ways.

1. It is written on the water and is gone before you can read it.

2. It is written with pencil and can be erased.

3. It is written with ink. A special substance is needed to erase it.

4. It is carved in stone and written in blood. It can only be expiated with deeply carved suffering and understanding.

The first two types of recording are generally acts of light-hearted carelessness, some little wound, an unkind joke, a thoughtless bit of character assassination. You feel sorry and—it is gone. The third is done with intention and is erased with difficulty. A special soul substance is needed such as deep, true compassion.

The fourth karma is cold sin, done without compunction. It is carved so deep in stone that no master, healer, or saint can help to remove this in one lifetime. The patient should understand that if his karma is caused by something that is written in blood, only a counterbalance through good karma accumulated in the passage of time can cure it. An enlightened healer can only point the way to awareness and the building of a clean future.

In such a case, what can you do? The wise healer will guide you up the steps that you must take in order to burn your karma.

1. You must become *aware*.

2. Feel sorry, not guilty but sorry.

3. Take positive action toward goodness.

4. Stay close to good people, those who have conquered most of their inner enemies.

5. Collect the blessing of holy, spiritual people. They are sent to help you, which is not luck but a grace from God. Watch for them, get in tune with them, and you will feel humble. In that way you are burning your ego also.

6. Repeat a mantra, such as, "I bow to all those who have conquered their inner enemies." As we bow in our hearts, hoping to reach the level of these conquerors, we learn to recognize our own inner enemies.

These are the actions you can take to wear out your adverse karma. Step by step, aware and disciplined, you will prevail.

It is *essential* to feel for and console people who are suffering from pain, poverty, misery, disease, lack of knowledge, or low intelligence. On whatsoever level you can, extend what help you can give, not out of fear of karmic retribution but from a flow of pure compassion. Be alert at all times to modify your karma, by *correct* thought and action.

Is the touch of the healer's hand necessary?

Not really, but sometimes out of love with no thought but to give affection and comfort as when a mother sooths her child and her hand is like a balm. In the same way, the holy man may say, "My daughter," or "my son," and place his hand on you, and you will feel better as he prays for you. That kind of touch motivated by affection always helps.

Generally, however, no physical demonstration is needed. The holy man can send his invisible vibrations any distance or anywhere that the person is situated who is in need of his blessings.

Can a scoffer be healed?

Yes, an unbeliever can be helped, in spite of his refusal to take the blessing seriously. The blessing is a beneficial vibration.

There are many who believe in an ethical life but cannot easily accept the logic of karma and the concept that illness has come to them because they have harassed somebody in the past. If it is at all possible, the healer should try to teach such people to be more than ethical, to be compassionate and devote more time to benefitting others. If they begin to live on that level, they will reduce the effect of the previous actions and feel better.

People like Hitler and others, who have massacred human life, may return as lepers or be forced to suffer horrible seeming injustice. In such cases karma can be compared to a toll bridge, and the patient cannot escape paying the toll even if he has taken a healer into his car.

Nobody can heal or cure any person with heavy karma that is carved in stone. He can only be helped to modify that karma by becoming aware and learning to build for the future from where he is now. The laws of the universe cannot be upset.

Can unconscious people, babies and animals be healed by the efforts of a healer?

His presence will help just as a healing light is good for all living things including plants. But it must be remembered that a sick child's spirit has chosen his illness.

We cannot believe that God is partial to a few healthy people and not to the children who are born in Vietnam, for example, where they suffer the effects of war, or in Africa where they die of starvation. Those who believe that God creates each life new minted and that all people come directly from his house do not have an answer to this cruel injustice. So we must understand the logic of karma and that we suffer for it whether it was accumulated yesterday or a hundred years before, and that in each life we are given an opportunity to redeem it. Christ said, "As ye sow, so shall ye reap."

The malefactor who believes otherwise gives himself

license. "I only live once," he thinks, "and I have already ruined any salvation I might expect. If there is any afterlife, my punishment is waiting for me, so I might as well go on this way." It is not punishment he will receive but a *logical consequence of his actions*, which he will have to endure and live out until he becomes aware. This is actually the greatest of mercies—not a chance to throw it all off and remain the same undeveloped man, but a *free tuition to a long course in compassion and wisdom*.

It is one of the beliefs that a holy man can take your karma upon himself. I do not agree, although there are reported incidents of this among some saintly teachers. But it is like telling somebody that I will eat instead of you. It is denying the other person the privilege of working out his own sequence of lessons. Therefore, I do not condone or even agree that it could happen since it goes against the natural laws.

In the old days there were some rascals who offered to take on karma for a large sum of rupees. Some fools actually gave them the money. People were also victimized in the cemeteries where the rascals would tell the children, "Your father has some very bad karma but I will help for a consideration. Give me a pocketful of rupees and I will write a note to God. All will be forgiven."

What is the most cooperative and ideal behavior on the part of the patient?

I would like him to understand that his soul is like transparent glass which his thoughts will either clear or blur. If he wants to maintain his well-being and reflect the strength and clarity of the spirit within, he must keep the glass clear of negative or harmful, uncharitable thoughts. One vicious idea can cover the transparency with particles which can only be removed by awareness and purifying actions. He should repeat often, "I am the transparency."

Karma-making in this lifetime.

I will go further into the subject of karma and the vibrations and reactions for good or evil that we are adding to ourselves in this particular lifetime.

Your body, together with the spirit that inhabits it, is like a sitar. If you do not understand the instrument, you cannot create music. You have learned your way around the world but you are still a mystery to yourself. If it were not so, you could perform miracles, for the human mind has an infinite resource which you have so far only encountered in vivid glimpses, short as heat lightning but held fast in the memory forever, for they were *the reality of your life's experience.*

All any teacher can do is show you the path. You have to walk it alone. You must find your own way, and for this you have been given great, pure guides. If Christ was to be born again, what could he tell you that he has not already told? What could he show you that he has not already shown? I do not understand why people are always waiting for Christ to be born again, or Buddha to return, and so on. They have already given us their instruction. We have the treasure map, the chart, and the compass. What more? Their mission is over. Now it is our mission.

Before we start out on it, we must understand what we carry with us, what is in our bodies and our souls, and the concept of the subjective mind and the objective mind. The objective mind deals with matter or your material, physical self. The subjective mind is like a mirror, a reflector returning to the body what you reflected in the mirror. Nothing will be sent back but what you have sent in. However, it may reflect upon you in a different way.

Psychologists refer to the conscious and subconscious mind and have many other names. You could think of it as the surface mind and the inner mind, but it is always the same old mirror into which you reflect your thoughts and actions, storing them away until they come back to reflect upon you and make you moody or sick according to the images you have given it.

I am speaking only of the karma we build from day to day in this one lifetime. It is action and reaction all the way. Your moods change according to the subjective mind's mirror reflecting its images on your objective mind. Be very, very careful of what you put into it.

Sometimes it happens that a man or woman can seem cheerful and normal just before going home to commit suicide. Something that had been fermenting a long time in his subjective mind, erupted and he lost all desire to live.

When a person feels unnecessary to anyone including himself, from that day, his life-energy begins to die. So if you would feel useful, and to feel so you must be so, learn to serve. Those people who serve mankind give energy and therefore receive it. Great people work hard and live long. Everyone senses the strong vibrations on those who give. Even their thoughts are blessings.

Somebody once asked me what my hobby was. I replied, "To collect blessings, the highest energy. A stamp collection, and so on, remains here on earth, but my col-lection of blessings can be transformed into pure energy and accompany me into the universe." When you help someone and that person speaks to you from the heart, saying, "God bless you," this is a valuable possession. Store it.

If you do nothing for anybody but yourself, if you really enjoy and take pleasure in the act of meting out death to living creatures in the more savage killing sports, if you behave cruelly to powerless people or have been generally careless and cold in your attitude toward others, you will become sick. A doctor can give you medicine that may relieve the symptons but create others. A healer can hypnotize you for a few days so that you will feel better, but you will not be healed, because inside the subjective mind you are all negative. The healer's influence remains for a little while then fades, because ultimately the objective mind must reflect the self-centered cruelty that has been mirrored upon it, and this reflection will result in disease or depression.

Your mirror receives and stores and, when the time comes, it sends back—"Take it away, I have stored it long enough!" So, if you have wished for somebody's illness or been pleased over his misfortune, then your objective mind has sent a thought of illness into your mirror. Sooner or later, your thought will be sent back, mirrored upon you.

A doctor, teacher, or healer will use different methods on you, none of which will work for very long. You may read books or listen to sermons that will tell you to think positively and be cheerful. This treatment may work well enough to banish your present discomfort, but as one form of your sickness goes another arrives. Forms change as you go from heart disease to back pain to high blood-pressure and so on. Just as long as the things that you have sent to the subjective mind are still there, so long will it keep on sending them back to you.

You must go to work on your mirror. There are four ways of consuming the kind of karma which you have accumulated in this life time.

1. *Recognize yourself.* You have done some things that are wrong; that is why you feel sick, out of rythmn. Do not stop with this thought. If you stop there you feel guilty, and if you feel guilty you will call yourself a sinner, and that is not good. It will reflect back in the mirror. Only become aware and recognize. To do this is to go forward, as you understand that you have acted and thought in ways that have not been good and they have worked through you like a boomerang.

Thoughts are living boomerangs and must be disciplined. When you downgrade someone else through envy or a desire to elevate yourself, remember the professor of mathematics who drew a line on a blackboard and asked his class to shorten it without erasing or touching it. Only one pupil could solve the puzzle. He drew a much longer line parallel to the original line. So stop any impulse to cut down another and instead draw a longer line for yourself.

2. *Pray.* Lift up to your higher dimensions. When you pray you are opening a window within yourself. Prayer means communication with your higher self. From that summit you can see endless vistas of light and energy. Einstein was able to contact the energy of the atom through his soul's energy.

3. *Connect.* You have communicated, you have opened the window and seen the infinite resource you have there. Now stretch out your hand, saying; "Let me have it." Go inside, let the light rush into you.

4. *Progress.* Walk forward in that light. For this you may need a teacher who can help you remain in contact with this higher energy within. In his company and with his influence, you are able to go further. When you falter, he lifts you—"Come on." As the music of a band revives a soldier, a teacher lifts your spirits in the same way.

To remain in a state of light and affirmation is very difficult. If you are with negative people and are out of sorts yourself, in a few days every gain you have made is gone. The teacher has painted beautiful things, but they are washed out as if a bucket of water had been washed over a water color. You must stay consistent and know that if you are in contact with the main thing, your higher consciousness, everything that you need will flow from it.

When you finally learn to know this most important personage dwelling within you, this king of kings, the healing process takes place. You accumulate no more adverse karma since the strength and measure of the kindness and compassion that you give will be reflected back to you from now on.

However if you have built a very sticky karma that is heavy with the glue of wickedness, an enlightened teacher will show you how to bear it with peace and balance. In the good company of your teacher, your sticky karma, which would guarantee you years of harassment, will be over in a shorter period, unless you have carved it in stone and blood, and then only time and humility can erode it.

So, the future is secure, the present is in awareness, and the past is being paid up. You must, however, keep yourself constantly tuned into the Sut Sun, which means the company of the eternal. A saint is considered Sut, because he speaks of the eternal. He feels its influence, knows its meaning, and is always in tune with it.

When you are in the company of the Sut Sun or the teachings of one of its masters, then you are moving ahead. When you know that you are positively moving, you are able to encourage yourself, and you need never feel solitary or depressed. You are in the company of the eternal. You have found your center.

That is why I say that your body, together with the spirit that inhabits it, is like a sitar. Now you can combine your duality and understand the action of the subjective mind on the objective mind. You are in tune, an expert. Since you understand the instrument, you can create the finest music on this sitar by uniting your vibrations into one harmony.

Harry Edwards

BIOGRAPHICAL SKETCH

Harry Edwards, one of the great healers of the world, was President of The National Federation of Healers in England and founder of the famed Healing Sanctuary, in Surrey, England. A distinguished author and lecturer, he practiced spiritual healing for over forty years. His case book abounds with the names of some of the most distinguished men and women in their various spheres, as well as thousands of others who responded to his remarkable healing powers. "Spiritual healing," he says, "no longer needs to be proven. It is factually established through the healing of the incurable."

He has conducted experiments in mass healing, absent healing, and in his own life lives the principles, simple yet profound, that govern all spiritual healing.

When asked how much of his amazing results are due to faith healing, he spoke of the natural healing intelligence of the body. "The body can lose its incentive when the illness becomes an accepted part of life and taken for granted. The healing purpose is to awaken within the patient's spirit the desire to be well. Any kind of faith is valuable here in sustaining the belief that it is possible to get well and thereby stimulating the bodily intelligence to get active and overcome body disharmony."

Harry Edwards' deep sincerity and thousands of well-documented healings brought streams of people from all over the world to his Healing Sanctuary. He also carried on a world-wide correspondence in which he demonstrated that healing at a distance is effective.

When we first visited the famous Healing Sanctuary of
Harry Edwards, a large, pleasant mansion in the coun-
tryside of England, we were permitted to sit right next to
him during an entire session in which he treated the people who had flocked to his healing presence. Though
Harry Edwards died a few years ago, his sanctuary and
healing methods are continued by his two able assistants,
Olive and George Burton, who assisted him while we
were there.

In his late seventies, Harry Edwards' beaming face
seemed ageless. He exuded vitality and warmth. When he
placed his hands upon an aching back or a crippled limb,
the expression of anxiety or pain on his patient's face
melted away, replaced by comfort and hope. Clearly, the
patient had been helped. Later, we asked one of his
patients to describe his sensations during a healing. He
said; "I felt an extraordinary warmth in the touch of
Harry Edwards' hands, and at times felt a definite
mystical current coming from his presence."

During our interview with him, Harry Edwards told us
that "Spirit Healing is not the perogative of any especially
endowed person but a common heritage of the whole of
the human family." He advises a student to *practice*
rather than try to learn and always to remember that the
healing power comes *through* us not *of* us.

He believed that healing is not the perogative of any
religion, race or gifted few but the common heritage of
the human family. "Healing may appear mysterious to
some people, but that is due to a limited understanding of
the way in which the healing spirit operates. A common
denominator links together all healing activities wherever
they take place, and that is the premise that healing is
God's gift to all his children, regardless of race or creed."

Harry Edwards insisted that there are thousands of
potential healers who could develop their gifts and, as a
result, bring relief and alleviation to the many whose

lives are racked with pain. His one criterion for the beginning healer is a deeply felt compassion for human suffering.

He believes that the healing purpose is not only to heal the sick but to awaken spiritual consciousness by demonstration of the power of the spirit in this materialistic and scientific world.

Harry Edwards Speaks

Before I gladly answer the list of questions put to me by Nancy and Esmond Gardner, I think it well that the postulates that govern the science of spirit healing should be clearly stated in order that the answers to the questions be understood.

Like all other forms of healing, spirit healing is a science, a spirit science, and healers should know something of this in order to cooperate intelligently with the healing process. Healers need to appreciate these fundamental postulates and laws which govern healing.

The source of spiritual healing is God, who created the perfect laws that govern life. Sickness follows the transgression of these laws.

The purpose of spiritual healing is to stimulate man's latent divinity, so that he lives in harmony with God's laws and, automatically reaping the result, fulfills the reason for earthly life. Spiritual healing, therefore, helps to accomplish the divine intention for man's spiritual progress.

The postulates which follow are concerned with the fulfillment of the divine purpose.

Every change in the universe is the result of law-governed forces. Nothing takes place by chance or without a reason. Thus our bodies are subject to definite laws which control our health from birth to the grave. Spiritual healing is the result of law-governed healing forces that induce change.

To effect any change purposefully, intelligent direction is needed to administer the law-governed forces to the subject. For example, man must direct the force of electricity to produce a given result within the laws which govern that force. The effective administering of a healing force requires intelligent direction.

Through spiritual healing, "incurable" patients are cured. The term "incurable" signifies that medicine can do no more, that earthly wisdom is exhausted, and the patient is condemned to suffer without hope of recovery. Thus when a spiritual healing succeeds with an "incurable," it denotes that a wiser intelligence than that of man is responsible for the law-governed, ordered change. If this intelligence is not earthly, then it must be of the spirit. The intelligent direction of a healing force originates from the spirit realm.

A diversity of human ills, from mental sickness to cancer, from nervous breakdowns to cataract, from blue babies to arthritis, are successfully treated by spiritual healing. This denotes that the directing intelligence is able to diagnose the cause of the affliction and to determine the correct character and strength of the healing force needed to remedy each given condition. In a successful healing, the directing intelligence is able to ascertain the cause of disease and knows how to administer the remedial force to induce a state of beneficial change within the patient.

There are physical laws which control the material world. As there must be order in spirit life, so there are spirit laws. The administering of a spirit healing force must conform to its laws, just as physical laws govern physical forces. The physical and spirit laws combined come within the definition of the total law. No healing is possible outside the confines of the total law.

One law is that harmony must exist between spirit, healer, and patient, between transmission of a force and its conscious or unconscious reception. Furthermore, the receiver must be in attunement with the transmitter.

The intelligently directed healing forces emanate from a non-physical realm. They are not physical, but through healership are transformed into physical effects. One function of the healer is to be the means, where necessary, for non-physical energy to be made physical. In contact healing the healer is the attuned receiver through whom the spirit healing forces are received for transmission to the patient.

When absent healing is effective, attunement is established between the healing intelligence and the patient. The healer's function is to be the communicative link between the absent patient and the healing source. In absent healing, the patient's spirit self acts as the transformer and receiver of healing forces through his spirit self. The spirit self can be in attunement with spirit intelligence, and he is therefore able to receive spirit direction and healing forces. He is also able to receive corrective thoughts and directives from the healing intelligence rightly to influence him and so overcome primary causes of disease. The patient's spirit self can also act as a receiver and transformer of healing force in contact healing as well as in absent healing.

For the alleviation and healing of physical ill-effects, the healing forces produce a changed chemical effect in the patient's body. This implies a profound spirit knowledge of chemistry and energies. The spirit healing forces, producing a planned chemical change, must, before the act of transformation, be synonymous with the energy-formations comprising physical matter.

These healing forces are able to create chemical changes through the application of one given form of energy to another. Beneficial chemical changes are also induced through the physical bodily intelligence.

The healing forces possess individual, particularized characteristics to effect beneficial change through introducing new factors that alter or disperse the harmful conditions. In cases of direct dispersal or induced chemical change, the effects are directed to the disharmony alone, and there is no interference with the healthy tissue or structure. This implies that the spirit intelligence performs an exact process, influencing only diseased cells or structures, without disturbing the healthy ones.

The establishing of this state of harmony is called "attunement." When a healer is in an attuned condition for healing, he is in a state of harmony with the healing guide, who is able to receive thought impressions from the healer and to give thought impressions to the healer's consciousness. This can be likened to a very slight degree of trance. It is through attunement that the healer becomes "conditioned" to be a channel through whom the healing energies flow.

What is the primary source of the healing power? Why is a human channel necessary to conduct the healing power?

Nothing takes place by chance in the universe. There is an orderly, reasoned process behind every state of change that occurs. This principle must apply to spirit healing too, but, whenever there is a planned process, there must be an intelligence which can use the law-governed forces to promote the change. Every healing must be a planned process, designed to bring about a change in either the outlook of the patient or in the affliction itself.

For example, if a person's joint is cemented together by arthritic adhesions, then those adhesions must be changed in their status to allow movement to come to the joint. To carry out a plan, an intelligence is needed to operate it. *When we see the healing of a condition that is said to be medically incurable, which means that human knowledge can help no further, it must mean that an intelligence superior to the human intelligence has come into the picture*, which can not only diagnose the source of the patient's trouble but also knows the means by which the right character of energy is applied to obtain the necessary chemical change in the person's locked joint.

This principle can be applied to all physical afflictions. With mental disorder, the directive guiding influences must reach the mind to cause a change in the outlook of the person and so help to overcome the primary cause of the trouble. The source of the healing must therefore be of a non-human nature, which we call spirit.

For a healing to take place, communication must be established by the healer with the spirit source of the healing. This is why it is necessary for a healer to have the faculty of establishing communication through attunement with spirit, to act as the means by which the healing is sought, and in contact healing to provide the means for the transmission of remedial energies to the patient.

Because there exists a state of communication between the realm of spirit and physical life here, there must be a medium which connects both forms of life. If that medium can basically be said to be energy, this can well be the clay and stone of spirit life as well as it is for physical life.

To effect a change in the chemical status of a part of the body, such as the arthritic joint, then the corrective energy must be an ordered arrangement of elemental atoms, structured into molecules which can change the status of the calcium carbonate, which is the principal agent of arthritic cement. When this is directed to the patient's joint, the change takes place, the status of the cement is altered, and the joint is freed for movement.

Obviously the human intelligence is necessary, first, to make contact with the spirit healing intelligences, and secondly to act as the channel necessary to convey the spirit-formed healing energies to the patient.

What is the difference between magnetic and spiritual and faith healing?

Spiritual healing is healing from spirit. This has no

direct connection with faith healing, which is dependent upon the self-determination and will-power of the sick person to get better. If all spiritual healing depended upon "faith," then we could not see babies, children, and third parties healed as they are. Faith healing is more likely to be associated with magnetic (or cosmic) healing. Magnetic is a wrong word to use to describe this process, but I will continue to use it for the sake of convenience.

Magnetic healing is the direction of his cosmic strength from a healer to a patient, to overcome weakness and to give him new strength and vitality to build up his resistance, and so assist him to combat the sickness. For the reasons that cosmic healing is associated with the cosmic forces that eddy round and about us, it pertains to the physical realm and not to the spirit. Cosmic forces can be taken into the body through the ductless glands, particularly the psychic gland which has its commencement at the base of the nose, and proceeds alongside the spinal cord, and thence continuous with the nerve network throughout the body. A typical example of cosmic force consists in the solar rays which give all living things the energy they need, i.e. the chlorophyll through the breathing of the leaves of trees. When we purposely respirate, with the feeling and knowledge that one is absorbing into one's reservoir the cosmic strength that is available, then we build up our energies tremendously. It is these energies that a magnetic healer has the ability to transfer to a weakened patient.

There is no special intelligence behind the transference of these energies, except that of the healer's good intention to help the patient to recover and gather strength and vitality. In this connection the transference of his cosmic energies into the patient can be extremely helpful. A magnetic healer should, however, be fully aware of the means by which he can replenish his energies, mainly through purposeful respirations, in order to avoid becoming depleted himself after a healing.

*Are these gifts mutually exclusive or can the healer use
any method at will?*

A person who is unable to attune to spirit can be a
magnetic healer, but not a spiritual healer. He need not
even be a God-fearing man. He is one who possesses
generosity in his nature and has the desire to help those
who are weak or suffering. It is, however, a general rule
that the spiritual healer, by virtue of his faculty of attunement, develops affinity with the source of healing and
would necessarily be brought into conscious or
unconscious contact with cosmic forces. His ability to use
the magnetic forces depends largely upon the degree of
his understanding of the science of spirit healing. He will
know when to direct cosmic energies to a patient to build
up his vitality and his good health tone, to enable him to
better respond to the spirit healing treatment. He may do
this subconsciously, as an interim treatment prior to the
purposeful seeking of healing forces from spirit to heal the
patient.

It is customary in some countries (especially in Europe)
to call spirit healers "magnetizers," and it is by this name
that they are known. It is my belief that many of
these healers are not only magnetizers, but they are in-
struments of the healing intelligences, which is quite a
different thing.

*Is healing an inborn gift or one that a dedicated student
can acquire?*

I would not deny the possibility that a person with the
gift of healing is the result of a spirit purpose. History
shows that at times when the interests of the human family are in peril, then a leader is born to help show the people the way to adopt a new sense of values and lead them
out of the impasse to which they have been heading. Of
course, the principal illustration in this connection was
the coming of Jesus at a time when Roman life was

deteriorating very fast, with debauchery, slavery, wars, and discontent.

The gift of healing can be developed by people who possess virtues of generosity, sympathy, compassion, and a desire to render service to the community in a spiritual sense—people who possess these characteristics and who then *inwardly feel* they have an insistent desire to be able to take away pain and unhappiness. Then they may well possess the latent powers of spirit healing, which only need a period of time to develop attunement and to give the gift an opportunity for expression. This desire to heal must come from the heart; an academic desire is useless. The gift of healing must fulfill in the person a desire to render service to God and to man.

The type of person who will never become a spiritual healer is one who is self-centered, mean, who will not render a service unless he receives some return for that service, someone who does not support good causes, one who is indifferent to suffering, and who possesses no love for the animal kingdom.

What qualities are needed to become a channel for healing?

This question has been largely dealt with in the previous answer. People can be divided into categories. There are the very materially minded individuals whose sense of values is bound up in material gain. They regard rendering service for love as weakness. Then there is the great mass of people who are generally apathetic and indifferent about concerns outside their own personal welfare, so long as they can live without being hindered or bothered by outside matters. Those who are content with their lot are negative to the spiritual healing directive. There is the third group I have referred to in the previous answer, who, in a social sense, are the pioneers of new humanitarian movements. One usually finds the consciousness of that which is "right" and that which is "wrong" as their motive power, encouraging them to work for good causes. They live by a high code of values, not necessarily religious ones, living according to their conscience, not knowingly doing harm to any other person, resisting cruelty in all its forms, whether to people, children or animals. They do not seek any personal aggrandizement or profit from healing the sick apart from the mutual happiness and satisfaction that healing gives to both patient and healer.

What disciplines would you recommend?

No disciplines at all, but avoid all "excesses." One can be an excessive smoker or drinker, and this is harmful. A healer should live naturally and freely, freed from restrictions, and be able to express in his way of living the quality of his healership.

I have heard that some healers fast before attempting healing. If a healer feels that this is an aid to his healing, then so be it. If a healer likes to play certain music before healing or while he heals, then he should do so. A healer should follow out his impressions. He should avoid ritual, avoid repetition, avoid being mechanical in any way, but be content to follow the impressions that he himself is conscious of receiving. He should put before the bar of common sense any movement or action that he takes, asking if it is necessary within the scheme of spirit science. He should ask himself if any form of ritual, which is nothing more than an exercise of the healer's mind, can help the healing intelligences to receive the simple message that the patient needs healing for a given complaint.

If there is one lesson that the writer has learned in more than forty years of spiritual healing, it is that, as far as the healer is concerned, it is a matter of utter simplicity. This is the hardest lesson for a healer, who is so anxious to heal the sick, for he wishes to do this himself and take a personal part in it. He is not content to act as a passive instrument through which the healing power can flow to the patient. If in healing a difficult condition the trouble yields only partially, the healer has to learn not to try to do further healing himself. He should know that he has not the healing intelligence which knows the way to administer the right energies which will make the given condition yield, in order that a satisfactory change can be made.

Is it necessary to make a diagnosis?

The simple answer is that it is not necessary, the reason being that it is not the healer who administers the healing treatment but the healing intelligence or guide. It is the healing intelligence that brings about the change for the better, and he must know what is needed and must make his own diagnosis in order to determine the right character and strength of the energies that are needed to overcome the cause and the symptoms of the trouble.

Of course in healing many causes of trouble are obvious, such as one sees as the result of a stroke and other forms of paralysis, as well as difficult movements through arthritis, very poor breathing, etc. The healer will convey to the healing intelligence that is listening the impressions that his mind receives from the appearance of the patient. No healing can be truly successful unless the cause of the trouble is overcome, for we comply within the inescapable law of cause and effect, and, until the cause of a sickness is overcome, then the symptoms will surely follow.

It is natural enough for a healer to desire to be the agent for the healing of a specific trouble, but he should always remember that the act of healing is putting into operation a spirit science of a far more involved character than the physical sciences known by medical men. Of course this is more easily seen when one considers the healing of an affliction or a disease that is medically incurable, which means that medical science and the wit

of man can do no more at present. This must mean that
when a healing follows and the ill condition is overcome,
a wiser mind has come into the picture, possessing the
knowledge of how to direct to the patient those remedial
energies needed to overcome the cause of the trouble.

When giving healing, a healer can become aware of
certain effects, such as that of "heat" or "cold," "vibrations," or, what is more important, intuitive thought and
direction. This intuitive direction usually needs the
experience of time and healing to make it clear. When the
flow of thought comes, even though the healer may not
be aware of its source, he should accept it without ques-
tioning, but at the same time keep all information in
reserve until there is substantial proof that it is factual.

Does unusual heat emanate from the hands of a healer?

Most healers are conscious of a feeling of heat, especially when in contact with certain diseased areas of
patients. The diseases are mainly those dealing with
arthritis, rheumatism, etc., and others where there is the
need for dispersal. It also occurs if healing is being given
for growths. *This heat is felt by the patient as well.* It is a
heat that penetrates into the body. It is interesting to note
that a healer may experience this strong heat condition
when his hands are in a certain position on the patient's
body, but if he moves the hands to another part of the
body, he will find that the heat is not there. Yet it returns
the moment that he replaces his hand over the affected
part.

It is also significant that, although the heat is felt so
strongly by the patient and the healer, if a thermometer is
interposed between the hand and the patient there is no
registration of increased heat. Therefore, the heat energy
that is directed in healing is not a clinical or physical
heat. Interesting implications arise. I have the view that
this heat can be of a much greater intensity in its purpose
than ordinary thermal heat. For example, when the

arthritic substance of calcium carbonate is subjected to a great physical heat, then a structural change takes place. With spirit healing, dispersal of the cementing of the joint can be instantaneous. The feeling of heat is so often felt by healers when treating arthritis that the possibility exists that the potential of the spirit-directed heat can have a much greater power than physical heat because it does no harm to the patient. One day research will contribute an answer to these unexplained problems of today.

Does the healer project an invisible healing light?

I have not heard of this before, nor have I been conscious of it. A word that is frequently used in healing is that of "healing rays." Some healers are said to possess a wonderful blue ray, while another has a golden ray, and so on. I question whether these are factual or rather the product of the wishful mind, even though it is unconsciously projected as if it is a truth.

Just remember the simple fact that it will take a given energy to overcome a given complaint. It is a matter of chemistry for the right amalgamation of elemental atoms and the energy they represent to come into contact with a similar mass of molecules that comprise the affliction. It is a matter of law that when the spirit-directed energies can make the physical change in a patient, then this follows regardless. This is common sense, and so the use of different colored rays by different kinds of healers is a fallacy.

Other imponderable questions can arise from this. Can a clairvoyant see, for example, colors associated with a particular type of energy, or is the "golden ray" for example clairvoyantly seen as representing magnetism or another healing force? But we are not answering imponderable questions, we are trying to deal with a factual situation.

Is a healer tired or refreshed after a treatment?

The act of healing should not tire a healer. Instead he should be invigorated because he has been used as a channel for the passing of energies through to the patient, and so would have received inner strength and vitality himself. Since the healer does not heal but is simply the conveyor of healing, then there is no reason for him to be fatigued through healing, unless he is using his own bodily and mental strength when he should not.

A healer can deplete himself if he is deliberately, even subconsciously, directing strength from himself into a patient. When a healer is conscious of being depleted, it means that he has been giving from either his reservoir of magnetic energies—this is the flow, as with magnetic healing—or he has been directing his own physical and mental strength to the patient. This he should not do. A healer should know that the healing effort comes *through* him and is not *of* him. Every healer should learn the way in which to restore depleted energies by characterized breathing, consciously taking into himself the cosmic energies that are there for his benefit.

It should be noted that at times a healer feels that he is consciously experiencing the symptoms and painful conditions of the patient. He receives these impressions through his state of attunement with the healing intelligence and the patient. Because of his state of affinity with the patient, who is recording his painful conditions as an experience of his mind, it follows that when the healer is in a state of affinity or attunement with the patient's mind, then the healer's mind can become conscious of what the patient is experiencing, and thus the healer receives a mental impression of the patient's suffering. These feel very real to the healer, but of course they are not factual. As a rule, as healing develops, then these experiences do not come.

Does the healer consciously raise his vibrations and generate psychic energy?

A healer can encourage his psychic awareness through meditation and development. The words "psychic energy" are not a definite term which can be described, any more than "psychic force" can be reduced to more definite terms. When a healer is in a state of attunement with spirit, then as a rule his physical energies quiet down; the active mind, which deals with mundane things, falls into the descent, while his spirit mind, encouraging spiritual thoughts and other thoughts of a high nature, becomes ascendant. Therefore, at a time of healing his "vibrations" should be of a much finer order and of a more spiritual quality.

Does the healer connect with a healing guide? A pool of cosmic wisdom? Or achieve oneness through prayer?

The answer to this question is yes to all three parts. There must be the spirit healing intelligence who is attuned to the healer in order to establish communication between the spirit realm and the physical realm. The term "a pool of cosmic wisdom" is, of course, applicable to the knowledge and experience that is contained within the phrase "a spirit healing science." This must take into account all the known forces, whether cosmic or more material, like the force of cohesion, gravity, magnetic attraction, and so on. In addition, the pool of wisdom must also contain knowledge of chemistry and the use of energies and of how energy can be applied to energy.

Concerning achievement through prayer, it must not be forgotten that healing is part of the eternal conflict between good and evil. Disease is evil. Illness is a cause of unhappiness, and therefore is not good. The origin of healing is God, who has given us his Laws of Creation by which we must abide, and from this receive either happiness or unhappiness according to our use of those Laws.

God is the center from which all healing flows. It is here for the whole of the human family, irrespective of faith, color or creed. It can never become the prerogative of any religion or sect. There is not one set of laws for the Catholic and another for the Mohammedan, for the Baptist, or the Spiritualist. They all tap into the fundamental laws of healing according to each one's progression and the ability to understand them. Healing is superior to all religions, for it matters not whether a person is a Mohammedan, a Sikh, Brahmin, or a Christian. They all respond in the same way to spiritual healing as does the Anglican and even an atheist.

Does the healing process differ for different problems, such as mental illness, deformities, viruses, arthritis, cancer, etc.?

As far as the healer is concerned, the answer is yes. Different healing processes are needed for different classifications of disease, and still further defined according to the patient's needs, intensity of illness, etc. It must be obvious that a different energy is needed for dispersing a cataract in the eye than for correcting a spinal curvature, or for an unbalanced mind or for overcoming an infectious disease.

It cannot be too strongly pointed out that every healing must be an individually planned treatment, requiring an individual diagnosis according to the state of the patient's affliction. It will take a given energy to bring about a given change. It is a matter of spirit science dealing with physical and thought chemistry. Each positive thought has its own energy formation, just as every degree of light and sound possess.

Are there any limitations on the healing process? Why are not all people healed at a healing session?

The only limitation is that the healing treatment must come within the scope of the "Natural Laws," i.e. the laws governing creation, birth, life and death. No healing can take place outside these laws, but within their scope much can be done. Still a healing may not be possible within the total laws which govern our well being.

Every person presents a different problem. With some, healing can be instantaneous; with others, especially with functional troubles, such as diabetes, epilepsy, and so on, time is needed for the healing to induce a beneficial change.

Is the healing treatment to be given only once to a patient or must it be renewed?

There can be no set answer to any question like this. With absent healing the healer does not even come in physical contact with the patient. One treatment is often sufficient for conditions where the cause of the sickness is easily overcome. For deep-seated and chronic conditions, a number of treatments is necessary and sometimes should be continuous, to prevent recurrences, i.e. with leukemia, forms of paralysis, and so on.

Will the healing process continue if the healer stops treatment?

My opinion is yes. There are so many recorded cures after a single treatment. One cannot imagine a spirit doctor giving up a patient he has been asked to help because the patient is not able to return for further treatments. This also accounts for sick people who progressively get better over a period of time, even though they do not see the healer again.

Can reasons be given for the failure of a treatment?

If a patient is losing keenness of vision and continues to overstress the sight by strain of very close work, the good which the healer can bring is negated. If a person suffering from rheumatism sleeps in a damp room, the trouble persists. Then there is the question of age and the slow breaking down of normality.

There must be a reasoned process to account for a non-healing as there is for a successful one. A general reason is that the cause is being maintained or has not been overcome. The law of cause and effect must apply.

To obtain a reasonable answer to this question, each case needs to be studied individually, the nature of the patient, his body, mind, and the cause and symptoms of the affliction. To fully answer could take a long while, especially when seeking to overcome the psychosomatic causes such as frustrations, emotions, and intellectual weaknesses.

Does the healer visualize the illness and then visualize it as cured, or does he visualize a perfect and healthy person from the start?

Healers work in different ways. There is no one way. He can view the healing need in either way asked in the question. My view is that the less occupied the healer is with his own thoughts, the better. The healer does not heal.

The key to successful healing is the faculty of attunement and intuitive affinity. With experience, the healer is intuitively informed of the diagnosis and the healing purpose, and then the healer knows what to look for, such as a spine to straighten. In this way there is cooperation between the guide and the healer for the patient's healing to take place.

Is the touch of the healer's hands necessary?

Strictly speaking, the answer is no. Absent healing proves this, especially for physical afflictions and diseases. On the other hand, the human factor should receive consideration. The healer can be used as an instrument for the direction of the healing energies. This is evidenced by the feeling of heat within the patient from the healer's hands.

The healing energies in the first place originate in the

spirit realm; they are the spirit counterpart of their physical form. There must arrive the time when the spirit energies are transformed into their physical counterpart in order to bring about the desired chemical change. The healer is in attunement with both spirit and physical and becomes the transformer, and thus can be used as the medium for the beneficial energies to be given to the patient.

In healing, the patient is the first consideration, and the personality and nature will differ with each one. There is, however, the class that can be psychologically helped, those who feel they need the healer's presence and his hands to "smooth" away pain and discomfort. There is the class of people who suffer from fears and need the healer's assurance that they are groundless. A psychological appreciation becomes part of an experienced healer's understanding and is indeed most valuable. But for healers who may not have this experience, he or she should let the hands be used upon a patient, according to his or her impressions, to fulfill the healing purpose.

What are the reported sensations of the patient?

One cannot give an answer to this question. Every patient is different; the disease is different and so is the intensity of the trouble. In general, however, *patients feel that they have new strength, with a freedom from anxiety*. If they have been suffering from sleeplessness, then sleep becomes more refreshing. Improvement is usually seen with the taking in of nourishment and especially with better respiration.

The patient invariably is conscious of having received help with the healing. The symptoms of stress lessen as the healing process is furthered.

Can the patient be benefited simply by his proximity to a healer without conscious volition on the part of the healer?

The answer is yes, especially if the healer is aware of the patient's need for healing in order to set the wheels of healing moving. Healing can never be a casual affair. It must have purpose and direction.

Healers are often able to inwardly know of the suffering a person is experiencing, and this awareness of illness becomes intuitive. Perhaps a reason for this is that the patient's spirit self knows of its healing need and is able to convey this information to the healer's spirit self, so directing his attention to the patient. It can be clearly stated that when a healer's sympathies are aroused for a person, then healing will take place to the extent that is possible.

It is well to remember that there is no evidence to suggest that healing reaches a patient automatically. Healing is a spirit science. To commence a healing treatment it is part of the law that there should be an invocation or intercession for the healing purpose to begin. This applies to all people, both primitive and more advanced, often taking the form of prayer or the act of seeking help for a sick person in a positive way, by intercession or in personal healing.

Can a patient at a distance, and unaware of the healer's efforts on his behalf, be healed?

The answer to this is a very definite yes. Absent healing proves it. If this were not so, we should not see children, babies, or animals healed. The same applies to third-party patients who are too ill to know anything about the healing effort being made for them. An example would be a person in a coma, or another person who has suffered a severe accident and is unconscious or in such distress that he would not be able to be aware of a healer's efforts. In such cases an immediate response for marked improvement can be timed or dated by the commencement of the application for the healing. This answer also answers the next question.

Can unconscious people, babies, and animals be healed by the efforts of a healer?

Babies and young children very often respond more easily and quickly to spirit healing than adults. This may be due to the fact that their minds have no fear of the sickness and they are less inhibited than adults. I believe that babies can be helped even before they are born, especially to overcome any tendency that may exist in the family for loss of a sense, such as sight or hearing. This implies a much wider field for research, to discover the extent to which genetic tendencies can be influenced by informed spirit guidance before birth. We have the evidence that genetic tendencies can be changed by spirit when we observe, as part of a plan, the change for the better of a person who is unloving, even sadistic—the change from inflicting cruelty and suffering into kindness and thoughtful consideration.

My last thought on this question is that, because babies and children and animals are excellent subjects for spiritual healing, it proves that healing must be a spirit science and is not just a result of faith.

Can a scoffer be healed in spite of his refusal to take the healing effort seriously?

The answer is yes. *Spiritual healing is superior to all of men's ideas*, "scoffing," conventions, or different religions. We have seen on so many occasions not only scoffers but atheists and others who have no religious feelings or faith respond just as readily as people who possess religious convictions.

Spirit healing does not exist exclusively for Roman Catholics, Protestants, Mohammedans, or any other section of people. It is God's gift to all His living creation. The views their minds hold pertain to earthly conceptions in physical life, but healing is of another (spirit) dimension. The views of the patient really have no association with the healing forces. This equally applies to the healing of patients suffering from mental conditions, as long as the mind is receptive to the thoughtful influencing and guidance from the spirit intelligences or guides.

What is the most cooperative and ideal behavior on the part of the patient?

The obvious answer is "to get well." We have to remember that the average patient knows very little about spiritual healing. It may be that he has received some hearsay evidence from someone else, or he has read an article in the press, or been advised by someone to get healing for his trouble; but on the whole he knows very, very little about spiritual healing and all that it implies.

The answer once again must rest upon the character of the disease the patient is suffering from. For example, if it is a kind of paralysis needing encouragement for the return of coordination, if a patient follows out the healer's advice in seeking encouragement for coordination through his mental direction, then that must be good. If, on the other hand, the patient deems his condition to be incurable and makes no effort at all, then the healing is limited. If the patient has been suffering from mental tensions and does not seek to help himself in the way the healer has advised, then the tensions are likely to continue and to dominate his being. If a patient is suffering from bronchial troubles and follows out the healer's advice on how to characterize his breathing, here again good progress can be looked for.

As a rule a patient goes to a doctor to get treatment, but he goes to a healer to get well. Therefore, he has the desire, and possibly faith and confidence in the healer, that he can be made well. This is good, for it implies cooperation with the healing intention on the patient's part.

The answer to this question, therefore, depends upon the nature of the trouble, the character of the healer's advice, and the measure of cooperation that the patient will give.

Brother Mandus

BIOGRAPHICAL SKETCH

Brother Mandus is the internationally famous founder of the World Healing Crusade, with headquarters in Blackpool, England. His work is based on many years of research into the laws of mind, personality, and spiritual truths in relation to physical and mental sickness and the healing of these problems. His outlook and experience are world-wide and ecumenical. The Crusade is not a church. It is essentially dedicated to help all churches, organizations, business, industry, prayer groups, and individuals to understand the mysteries of the mind and the infinite power of meditation and prayer.

Brother Mandus is the author of many books and the voice in a large collection of tape recordings, as well as the publisher of two magazines. One of them, *The Crusader*, is sent free to all who ask. All this he considers "a miracle, because it could only have happened through the movement of the spirit working in and through our love, dedication, and commitment."

Traveling around the world, lecturing, and conducting Divine healing missions in churches and organizations, Brother Mandus draws crowds of people waiting for the luminous force of his words and person.

We met Brother Mandus on one of his world-wide tours. After he finished speaking, we were among those who requested his blessing. We watched this tall, fine-looking man coming down the aisle, placing his hands upon the heads of those who awaited his healing touch. He seemed to radiate goodness. When he paused and his hands rested lightly on our heads, he closed his eyes and let the healing power flow through him. Our sensation was that of relaxed certainty that whatever was in store for us, now or after our death, it was *all right!*

Brother Mandus conveys a confidence that strengthens the body's own healing powers. He firmly believes that we all can develop the ability to help each other by invoking a strong current of compassion and love that will flow through us to a suffering person.

Brother Mandus said of our book, "I am sure many people will be helped by having such a wide range of experience by different people represented to them in the form you contemplate. For my part, my life and work are dedicated to helping anyone and everyone into a great awareness of spiritual principles."

We often think of the words Brother Mandus spoke as he took leave of us. "May all those whose life touches you be blessed because you pass their way." These words epitomize his life.

Brother Mandus Speaks

In attempting to answer these profound questions, I think I should make my own position clear so that any assessments may be made in the light of my own experience in the past thirty years.

Right from the initial compulsion to begin this work, my only vision was based on research into the validity and effectiveness of spiritual principles insofar as I could perceive them and activate them. We did not establish a church or a movement. Down all these years the outlook of myself and my colleagues has been essentially ecumenical, working with other churches and organizations, constantly experimenting in the field of love, faith, prayer, and expectancy.

Our work inevitably moved beyond physical healing as such, because the deeper we probed the more surely we discovered the reality of the spirit of man functioning through consciousness, and that thoughts were indeed living things. Out of this research into human behavior patterns, the causes of mental and spiritual disease, attitudes in relation to problems, etc. came the need to share our experience with others in a very humble but, we believe, very simple and accurate teaching method.

With all this in mind I would like to emphasize that any comment made on these questions can only be offered in a very humble and inadequate way. Truth in all the facets and aspects of human behavior, spiritual principles, and prayer recedes into infinity. One reaches a position of understanding only to realize immediately that there is a new horizon beyond. Like attempting to define God, the Christ, divinity, cosmic consciousness, we are dealing not with a knowledge of ultimate truth but rather one of increasing awareness and discovery.

I emphasize this because in my humble view I believe it is imperative. In this whole field of research and adventure (for that is what it is) we are moving into new dimensions of thought and experience. This can only be accomplished in our day and age, in the midst of a great acceleration of the evolutionary process, by helping each other to be very flexible in our thinking, and totally ecumenical in all our concepts and dogmas.

I believe that we are rapidly moving towards an awareness and acceptance that no one group, no one church, no one religion has it all, either in precept or experience. For too long we have witnessed the terrible confusion and often conflict throughout the religious scene, world-wide. There is an urgent need for a new understanding of the great Law of Love and therefore a total acceptance of the universal nature of man that abides and is fulfilled in the Fatherhood of God. This transcends every closed mind and narrow doctrine. It leads inevitably into new dimensions of thought and experience.

As always, the individuals, groups, and nations can only progress according to the light of their visionaries. The need today is to lift our vision to the true significance of divine healing and feel the impact and necessity of full obedience to spiritual principles by which alone so many of our basic problems can be healed.

Perhaps the greatest contribution in the field of divine healing is that it breaks down barriers between religions and denominations. When by experience one finds healings taking place in every kind of situation, from a group of Africans on a hillside to a sophisticated church in New York or London, without any regard to the definition of religion or denomination, one is impelled to realize that we would be wise to move much more freely across the religious or spiritual field, knowing that the Lord is there, whether we are prepared to recognize him or not.

I therefore submit these thoughts, very tentatively, and knowing, despite a massive experience down the years, that whatever is suggested by myself or others, the total movement can and must only be towards greater research and experience. We must understand that the movement is through an infinite plane and therefore can only be progressive rather than final. And, if I may say so, one great warning to keep in the forefront of every attempt to explore this area of healing is that it is essentially not an intellectual process but becomes progressively more effective to the degree that *love* expressed in *compassion* concentrates every approach to it.

I believe the common denominator through the whole healing experience on earth, including the entire teaching and example of Jesus Christ, is the indefinable *Love Factor* which transcends consciousness and perhaps which ultimately is the basic motivation of life itself. With great humility and tremendous enthusiasm and, I hope, vision, I submit some thoughts in relation to the questions posed.

What is the primary source of the healing power?

The most significant and startling experience in my life came about without any personal motivation. Although I had long been aware of a simple method of meditation, just being still, I could not claim to know very much about spiritual teaching as such.

One day, quite some time before this work of healing began, I was helping my wife wash the dishes and actually, while putting the knives and forks away in the sideboards drawer, I had what I can only describe as an illumination. I was swept through and through with the most brilliant light I had ever seen. It was like looking straight into the noon-day sun, or the blaze of an electric welding arc-light. As best one can describe an indescribable experience, it seemed that I was dissolved in that light. It was an ecstacy, filled with an infinite and pulsing dynamic.

I had an awareness of infinity. The entire essence was absolute perfection. In that second I knew the interrelationship of all people, all life, all things, all worlds, and the entire universe. There could be no separation, but only a total unity in the almighty Spirit of God, the Creator, the essence of infinite perfection.

I knew without doubt that, had I been deformed or ill or in need of any kind, in that flash of perfection I would have been instantly healed. I knew there was only God, only almightiness, only eternal life, and that I was part of it, together with everyone else everywhere.

The light suddenly disappeared and I was left blazing with the memory of this transcendental experience, with the knives and forks still in my hand, which I simply proceeded to put into the drawer. Then life just went on as it apparently always had without any dramatic change of any kind.

I had been a business man all my life and, when the war came, like everyone else in Britain, I was conscripted. After the war, as soon as I could get free, I had a wonderful opportunity to establish a new business.

Deep within me was this tremendous feeling of becoming free enough to do something of a spiritual or social nature, without knowing what it could be. I entered into a business with the hopeful commitment that it would create enough money to look after my wife and two children so that I could very soon be free of the business to do whatever needed to be done. Perhaps this prompting was to offer some kind of compensation for the terrible tragedy of the war through which the world had passed.

I had to travel forty miles each morning to set the new plant in operation. I called at an Anglican or

Episcopalian Church every evening to pray. In five months, I realized that the business was crashing. All my life's savings had gone to nothing and I would have to close down immediately.

When I set off for home that day of decision, I went into the little church as usual, knelt at the altar and told the Father that the business along with my savings had vanished. What could I do now?

It was at this point that another miracle happened. Somewhere up among the stained glass windows behind the altar I heard three loud "cracks," like a clapping of hands. Startled, aware of some extraordinary event, I heard, subjectively, the "still small voice" which had complete authority. In effect, "Now, my son, your time has come. Now you have no money, nothing to support you. I want you to open a Sanctuary of Divine Healing in the name of Jesus Christ and rely upon me for everything." That was all. Then a wondrous peace and an awareness that entirely new adventures were opening out.

How to open a Sanctuary of Divine Healing? Without any knowledge or experience, I simply followed through as best I could.

I put an advertisement in the local newspaper: "Wanted, church, hall, room, suitable for conducting a Ministry of Divine Healing in the name of Jesus Christ." I got one reply. It was from an old lady. She had a great story to tell. A few months before my advertisement appeared, a small private hotel came on the market. She felt a strange compulsion to buy it. She did not want to run it as a business but felt a need to be able to visit and sit about in the place where she had lived all of her married life.

One day she was in the long dining room with her niece, and the niece turned to her, apropos of nothing, and said, "Auntie wouldn't this make a lovely healing sanctuary." A week later the old lady saw my advertisement and wrote to me. A week after I met her I was installed in a very adequate Sanctuary and waiting rooms.

So I had a Sanctuary and a Ministry of Divine Healing. I think my business and war-time training came to the fore and turned out to be a factor in managing my Sanctuary, in that I had the sense to realize who was in command. Quickened by the illumination from quite a long time previously, I knew that the infinite spirit of God did not need me to tell Him what to do or how to do it. Here I was, obviously placed in this position by some kind of inner compulsion, and therefore my relationship should be rather one of a servant being available to the Master. And it has been just like that, from that day to this.

I spent the first two days just being quiet, in meditation, in the presence of the Lord. The third day a crippled lady arrived. She said she had heard about this new Sanctuary of Divine Healing and wondered if she could get some help. She had been crippled for many years with arthritis, locked knees and shoulders and arms, and was constantly in great pain. There is always a first time for every new adventure, and I remember, very vividly, with a beating heart, talking to her and trying to find words which might help. I talked about the teaching of Jesus Christ, about prayer, so far as I could define it, and about being with the Father and what could happen.

The strange thing was that beyond the words I felt this overwhelming compassion towards her. I felt a great excitement that some wonderful good was happening because I saw her face lighting up. She was receiving something of this blessing through the words and this indescribable feeling of love.

Eventually I led her down to the altar. As she sat, I stood behind her and prayed. How does one pray? Well, I only asked the Father to bless and help her and we went into the silence in the presence of God.

Then, suddenly, with an excited voice, she said, "Oh, praise the Lord. I'm healed!" She got on her feet and quickly walked around the Sanctuary. She raised her arms. She was full of excitement. She had been instantaneously healed of a condition which all human skills had not been able to overcome for so many years. I simply looked at her with wide-open eyes, startled, before such an extraordinary miracle.

When she had gone I sat down in the presence of the Father. And in that moment I knew something which I have never had cause to retract throughout all these years. In that moment I had seen an invisible, almighty power floodlight a broken life and bring it into instantaneous wholeness. I therefore knew that man, and an inexperienced man in my case, could speak to the Lord and establish communion in such a way as to release this divine perfection.

I realized that this must be everyone's ability because the only factors observable to me had been simple prayer, inadequate knowledge, simplicity, and compassion for someone in need. I also knew, in those moments, that somewhere in this direction, with man in communion with his Creator, must lie the general state of well-being and health and infinite good — that this should be perhaps the natural state of man — that divine healing could in a way hold the "be all and end all" objective of spiritual experience or Christianity. I saw quite clearly that in this whole area of spiritual experience must lie the *prevention* of so much human disease and disaster, and that, in the end prevention was even better than miraculous cure.

Beyond that again I knew in that illumined moment that somewhere in this direction must lie the full fruitage of human experience. I saw that man was destined to be little less than the angels, that he would some day enter into a full and marvelous partnership with the Lord to be effective on every creative, artistic, and scientific level. I saw that here was the true science of life, and that the incredible and eternal future of man was already secure. He was only in process of unfolding his highest and eternal good as quickly as he could become aware of it.

I felt guided to write at some length here about my own experience only because it provided, for me, the essential awareness of the living presence of God in whom we live and have our being. The primary source of healing power, especially in relation to miraculous healing, obviously must flow from some awareness of divinity, almightiness, or that which is beyond human experience.

In my case it had been simplified to me and, thank God, gave me additional necessary vision to realize that communion with God had nothing to do with special gifts as such. This truth must be available for everyone without any exception. I think I saw even then that divine healing itself could not be circumscribed and that, could one discover and apply the great laws which govern communion with the Father, then obviously everyone could be in effective manifestation on behalf of everyone else and, of course, for one's self.

I proclaim my own central belief as an understanding, basic and effective in my own life and work. It became the true foundation of all the research work down the years, the discovery of the Law of Expectation, the experience of healing right across the world, the proving that distance was no obstacle, the recognition of man as a spirit functioning in consciousness and the physical system more like a machine than anything else.

Yet, I repeat it, I emphasize it, there are, so far as methods are concerned, probably as many ways to God as there are people on earth. In other words, the great lesson of my life is that I respect and am absolutely one with all those of every denomination, religion, or organization who in their own way are involved in seeking to help humanity. My only plea is that we might all be one together and thus know we are contributing to the total whole of man's experience. That is why our work is known nowadays world-wide as an entirely ecumenical and research work, with no "axe to grind," no conditions, just loving fellowship and friendship in prayer to share with everyone everywhere.

From that base I think I can more adequately attempt to express some thoughts in relation to the various aspects of the questions raised.

Why is a Human Channel Necessary to Conduct the Healing Power?

I believe that the great gift of God to man is that, although we are part of the one spirit, the one *Divine Mind*, we have relative free will within the overall and eternal will of God. We could not even be individuals without this right of choice. We create our personalities by the kind of thoughts we have. We choose our thought and action and reaction to environment as we see fit and within the light of our knowledge at any one time.

We all make many mistakes and observe the penalties for our wrong thinking, our violation of divine laws. We observe that when we are positively oriented, when we are filled with love, things are better. In other words, we are personalities in our own right within the universal mind or spirit. In fact, each person at any point in his or her life is basically a product of all thoughts since the moment of miraculous birth into this environment, plus the essence of the thought and experience of our forefathers. I feel that we all need to know and believe in the significance and responsibility of this free will. It is so easy to lose sight of true spiritual values by rebelling against difficult or dark experience.

People often say to someone like myself: "Yes, all this spiritual truth is very beautiful, but why talk to me about a God of love when millions of people have been killed in war, when children are born maimed through some wrong drugs, when murders and violence and all these terrible things take place? Where is this God of love? Why doesn't He stop it?"

It is certainly true that we live in a world of great turbulence and are besieged with every kind of problem, disaster, disease, and man's inhumanity to man. What is not understood is that free will in itself carries a tremendous responsibility. We are here to learn how to live, how to use our thinking capacity to create good situations, and how to develop the most ideal personality. If God could just intervene and cross the boundary of our personal free will, then we would simply be puppets. We could not be individuals in our own right.

Beyond even the personal responsibility and choices of free will, there are also the national and world collective aspects of the same free will functioning throughout the social structure. In other words, it is man's individual or collective choice which sets wars into motion. It is man who comes into conflict with his neighbor and perhaps burns his heart out. It is man who so often chooses a violent course, or a drug scene, or becomes involved in worry and stress which can tear down the physical structure.

It is necessary, therefore, to realize this great truth in order more adequately to realize how our own minds are vital in the release, through prayer, of divine action into the midst of the healing scene. Here again, to the degree that we become complicated or uncertain or inhibited, to that degree do we perhaps constrain the full movement of the spirit in response to our prayers. I think that that is why Jesus talked so much about absolute love, a great simplicity of faith, and an acceptance that prayer means the release of infinite perfection into any situation. We have to make the choice of the degree of faith, the degree in which we recognize the Almighty Spirit. All these factors come into manifestation according to the level we know them to be true.

There is one other reason why a human channel is often very valuable. Since love is the flux, the continuous flowing of union with God and union with other people, there seems to be an all-consuming yearning in the spirit to establish deeper and more harmonious and happy relationships between people. That, after all, is the very essence of the Christ teaching and the essence of all religions on earth.

It is significantly true that when people are in serious trouble, whether of sickness, or intense worry, or catastrophe, it is very difficult under the pressure of the situation calmly to contemplate and believe in the infinite peace and perfection of God shining in their midst. The pain tends to blot out the calm awareness of infinite perfection. The conscious mind takes up the pattern of the imperfect and finds great difficulty in serenely observing and accepting the instantaneous presence and perfection of God as the complete answer.

People, often thousands of miles away, write in or make contact asking for help. The healer and the people in our Sanctuary become still before the Father and pray for the sufferer. This prayer in unison seems to be one of the great methods of divine healing, bearing the one in trouble up into the midst of God and really believing and knowing that because we are in prayer, something wonderful is set into motion. At that point the movement of the spirit can take over and sometimes produce an instantaneous healing, more often a progressive healing, and whatever else, a movement of infinite and multiplying good to help the person on the level of his or her need.

What is the Difference Between Magnetic and Spiritual and Faith Healing?

I would find it very difficult indeed to differentiate. There is always the temptation to define, to isolate, to bring in intellectual assessments, and I think that can often lead to many unnecessary difficulties. If there is one danger, I suggest it might be the development of ideas that healing has to do with human skills as distinct from being channels through which the infinite perfection of God can shine.

There is, in truth, an overall healing principle which is constantly at work. We live in the midst of miracles as part of the life structure itself. A cut finger heals by an inward process of the spirit motivating the various cellular structures of the body. The entire system has its own inbuilt, subconscious and conscious motivations towards the maintenance of health and well-being and the healing of sickness when it arises. Spiritual healing, in all its forms, merely moves to a higher dimension of consciousness which often greatly accelerates the natural healing process. Increasingly, and with ever more intensive awareness, I realize that all is spirit, all is consciousness, and that this is the basic factor in all healing of mind and body.

In this sense I cannot adequately attempt definition of these various aspects which other people with much greater authority in their own experience may be able to define.

Are These Gifts Mutually Exclusive or Can the Healer Use Any Method at Will?

I am aware, of course, that many people in many ministries adopt or are involved in a vast variety of healing techniques. It is also interesting to note that healing takes place in all these ministries! It would seem, therefore, that there is no exclusive pattern. It would almost seem that the moment anyone opens an aperture of love, faith, prayer, or awareness of something beyond human power, then the spirit floodlights through the aperture to help and bless, irrespective and regardless of the definition of the healer, the method, or the technique.

It is this factor, of course, which induces each individual or group to deepen faith in their own particular method and experience. The only danger is that we then sometimes tend to exclude the other people with their differing methods, and sometimes get into conflict about it. It is wiser to be totally ecumenical and to give thanks for all people who are seeking to help everyone else, knowing that the Father might even wish to use many methods.

Can Anyone be a Healer?

I believe, completely, that healing is everyone's ability and facility. I have spent my life in dedication to this proposition. All our research in the Sanctuary down the years has been devoted to this one end.

If it were true that only certain few people had "gifts of healing" then I, personally, would not wish to be involved in any concept or experience of it. From a true, spiritual point of view, in the light of man living in and through and by the spirit of God, it simply has to be true that all God's children on earth, irrespective of race, color or creed, must have this central ability to love and be loved, to be in communion with God, to make their choices, and to discover their own high destiny.

I believe it to be urgent that we dispel all these ideas that only certain few people can be channels of healing. For centuries it has been a basic belief that healing was only vested in certain few chosen people. I believe it to be a tragedy that such ideas were ever held. It is this concept that has probably done more to inhibit the churches in the full movement of divine healing than anything else.

In my experience, prayer and divine healing are one and the same thing. I agree that it is true that certain people seem to be raised up to fulfill a ministry, but they are merely the way-showers. When one considers the universality of the spirit of God, there should be no mystery about this since there is only the one flux of Divinity manifesting in everyone of the four billion people on earth.

At Divine Healing Services in many countries I have gone to great lengths to destroy the illusion that only certain individuals, like myself, have healing power. For this purpose I have constantly exemplified, for example, the unified prayer power of an entire congregation released in prayer on behalf of the sick who have come to the service. Time and time again one will witness an instantaneous healing. Someone will get up and walk out of a crippled or sick condition. Not, I emphasize, by the special prayers of a gifted healer but by the compassion of a congregation focusing their attention upon the perfection of God shining in the life of someone afflicted.

Is Healing an Inborn Gift or One That a Dedicated Student Can Acquire? What Qualities are Needed to Become a Channel for Healing? What Disciplines Would You Recommend?

I can only say in all humility that it is an experience which anyone can move into according to the degree of belief and acceptance.

The main problem is that most people believe in their inadequacy. Even though this gift belongs to everyone, relatively few people place much faith in their own ability to pray for someone else with any particular expectation of miracles happening in the one for whom they pray. The real need in these days is to help sweep away this sense of inadequacy, this uncertainty factor.

The essential qualities for healing, I emphasize again, are a great love for God and love for people. Healing takes place on the wavelength of *loving*. Jesus recognized instantaneous union and communion with God on a wavelength of compassion, which is love in action, the perfection manifested in instant healing. Love is the key to all healing. Therefore if one seeks to be a dedicated student, if one seeks to be a channel for healing, then one must be essentially a channel for love. The greatest miracle of all is that, irrespective of our intellectual education, we all have this flame of love within us. This is the factor to cultivate.

Disciplines? Again the only real discipline is to be eager and ready and willing to be expendable on behalf of people in need. Dedication to the Father, love for God, a belief in miracles, and an acceptance that wherever one goes with love we can be absolutely sure that the Lord has already gone before us.

Love is the discipline of being expendable. It is the discipline of selflessness. It is the discipline of not really seeking anything for ourselves. It is the ideal objective to offer our lives in total surrender to the Lord so that He may take us up and use us in His service.

Most of the trials and tribulations of the world, the greatest tragedies, are basically self-made. From warfare right on through to personality conflicts, man's inhumanity to man, fear and worry, stress and strain, bitterness, grief, broken relationships, boredom, all these and other aspects of human personality expressed in pain and problems, all these factors so often represent our deviation from an acceptance of the great Law of Love, deviation from the Christ ways of love, faith, prayer and service.

It turns out that the great majority of human ills would be healed, and this includes the causes of much disease and disaster, which would be healed when everyone knew, as an urgent concept of life, that we must not depart basically from the great Law of Love which is the secret of the balanced and harmonious life. The great Law of Love has to do with the total well-being and the safe progression of all mankind into the infinite future. This applies to the individual, to nations, and indeed to the world family.

What is the Healer's Procedure?

In our work as intercessors for help and healing we are, of course, involved in many and various situations. Our entire concept, as already described, is based on great love for people in need, simplicity of faith, and prayer which really accepts that something wonderful is set into motion.

In this sense we believe we can reach people worldwide. Everyday in our Sanctuary hundreds of letters arrive from all over the world. To each of these friends we send a letter in reply, often giving counselling and help in their need. We send free literature and ensure also that they receive our free magazine, the *Crusader, Power Lines,* and tape recordings or anything else which can be of help.

These letters from people in need are placed on the altar in our Sanctuary of Divine Healing. Everyday all our staff members gather in the Sanctuary at nine o'clock in the morning to link up in simple love and prayer for all of those people. We accept, and know that the Father does not need us to tell Him anything about any one of them. He was there when the letters were written. He knows all about each and every need. I believe that the Father has inspired each of these friends to write for help. Obviously He must know that, by involving us as a chan-nel of help, then He is able to release whatever is necessary for the well-being of each person in the right way and at the right time through their willingness and because we are linked together in love. It is certainly true that wonderful things happen through these interces-sions. We are linked with a world chain of prayer-partners.

One often has the experience of entering into personal intercession for the individual who may, perhaps, have called at the Sanctuary. In this case we are obviously in-volved in counselling, listening to the needs of the person, seeking to help clear away any uncertainties, and to quicken a dedication to the fulfillment of spiritual prin-ciples in that person's way of life.

It becomes very clear on so many occasions that the healing was not a physical need as such. The outward pains, pressures, arthritis, heart conditions, or whatever, very often are the outward manifestation of some inner turbulence, some unforgiven situation, some stress or worry or tension. It is certainly a fact of life that deep emotional and intensive disturbance in consciousness, so often through relationship problems, can produce devastating effects in the physical system.

It is with this thought that we then look very carefully to the counselling aspect of healing. It seems to me that we are not really healing anything if the *cause* is not healed. It often turns out that it was the *person* who needed to be healed rather than the machinery-body! So often when these inward conflicts are redeemed, repented, forgiven, released, then the body flows effortlessly and sometimes spontaneously into its natural state of well-being and balance.

A third procedure in which we have been intensely involved on world-wide missions is the Divine Healing Service in a church or hall or wherever a group of people can assemble. My interest has always been to teach and encourage the people to follow through on these spiritual truths. I seek to encourage the dedicated process to be applied in daily living.

I seldom even approach healing without some quite substantial teaching. It would almost seem from a healing point of view that my particular mission is to chip away many of the limitations which prohibit the well-being of a person and often help clear away the doubts and uncertainties in relation to prayer and the power of God in action. On all such occasions, therefore, I usually speak for half-an-hour or so and cultivate by recognition an awareness of the presence of God in our midst.

I lead into prayer. I gather up the resources of all the people and intensify them through an expression of love towards God and recognition of His presence as a living reality.

Then I call for people who would wish to be prayed for, and encourage the congregation to be quiet for a moment or two, believing in God's perfection shining in that person's life. At that point I will help to recognize that perfection in the sick person. So often the sickness disappears, or a new quickening of the spirit takes place.

On most of these occasions *people* are doing the praying and there is no laying-on-of-hands in that particular approach. At other times, as in a church with an altar, it is customary to have people come up to the altar. As they kneel, I pass down the line laying my hands of each head, knowing and believing in the silence that God's perfection is shining through to bless and heal.

Is It Necessary To Make A Diagnosis? If So, How Is It Done?

There are two aspects to a question like this. First, in all situations like counselling, one is in effect diagnosing in the sense that one is becoming aware of the needs of the person. The patient will describe his or her pains. We will be told about the tribulations and problems that have been part of the patient's experience.

It is certainly true that such discussion brings in an inspiration factor and very often a very clear awareness of the real cause to be healed. In this sense diagnosis is one of inspiration and communication. Then one is guided to release the situation to the Father and make way for prayer and the release of God's love, God's perfection, into manifestation.

Secondly, I know that many healers have a psychic ability to diagnose. They become aware of someone's pain, the cause of it, or whatever diagnosis is necessary to reveal the trouble. This is obviously some psychic faculty, some sensitivity, which can be very effective. I personally have no experience of it on this level.

Does Unusual Heat Emanate From The Hands Of A Healer?

Very often in contact healing, the laying-on-of-hands, one does become aware of heat. Sometimes the awareness is one of tingling, like electricity. Sometimes it is a coolness. Sometimes there is only a great peace in which one is aware that something wonderful is happening.

The patient, too, is often aware of these same sensations. On the other hand, quite often the pain or problem will disappear without any particular feeling at all.

Does The Healer Project An Invisible Healing Light?

The great help I personally had was the illumination, the Baptism of Light, which I experienced as described. This gave me quite naturally an acceptance and awareness of the presence of God.

In the quietness which I always instinctively know to be the stillness of God, the silence of the spirit, I simply accept completely that God's perfection is shining in the life of the person for whom I am in prayer. I find it helps me to quicken my imagination, my awareness, by realizing consciously that God in His own Spirit is and must be Instantaneous Perfection. This at least helps me to be a channel accepting almightiness as a reality. I am sure this awareness is transmitted also to the patient through my own definition in words of prayer.

Is A Healer Tired Or Refreshed After A Treatment?

Personally I am invariably very happy, refreshed, inspired. After a long Divine Healing Service, for example, I am really in a state of exaltation and humility and gratitude. There is indeed a tremendous sense of joy that a mere man could have been used to bring loving help to someone. It is a high privilege indeed to be of service.

Does The Healer Consciously Raise His Vibrations And Generate Psychic Energy?

As already stated, I consciously accept God's presence. I find the definition of instantaneous presence and perfection helpful in this sense.

Although prayer itself must generate psychic energy, I do not go into any kind of definition beyond the simple attitudes of love, faith, prayer, and recognition, as described.

Does The Healer Connect With A Healing Guide? A Pool Of Cosmic Wisdom? Or Achieve Oneness Through Prayer?

All these thoughts have basically been answered in the comment given previously. There is, of course, one other factor which has a bearing upon what many healers describe as their "healing guides." I repeat and emphasize our real need to be very ecumenical in outlook in every way. True spiritual foolishness lies in the direction of condemning anyone else in his or her own particular field of activity. Perhaps in a healing ministry, as in none other, the concept of being able to judge others tends to be dispersed by the universal nature of God's love in action through anyone who cares to be a channel of service.

I have no difficulty whatsoever in believing that, for example, there could well be a Heavenly Host helping at a Divine Healing Service. I have no difficulty in believing that shining ones on the next plan of vibration, or even loved ones, can come into the atmosphere of prayer to help someone on earth in the healing scene. I just know that life is eternal, that we all move on to a high realm, and that since love is the governing factor of the universe, I see no difficulty in love flowing from the higher plane to the lower and thereby people being able to help friends on earth.

For myself, I am not clairvoyant and have no direct experience of healing guides as such. I only believe the possibility and potential of such help. My whole attention is stayed upon God, and I find this better for me because it keeps me quite simple in my attitude, I do not have to be troubled by training psychic gifts, developing psychic faculties, or anything like that. I am content to know that the Father knows it all, and if He cares to send a thousand Archangels to help, then this is His concern and not mine.

In all ways I seek very simply to follow the full life and teaching of Jesus Christ in the knowledge that all these factors of spiritual reality are really leading all mankind, irrespective of religion, towards the full brotherhood of man in the one Fatherhood of God.

What Is The Healing Process?

I believe the real healing process is the floodlighting of a person's life, in mind, soul, spirit, body, and circumstance, with the perfection of God. I believe God's love fully released will bring about a perfect divine adjustment in a person's life pattern.

The process itself must be of divine origin. The Lord knows what to do and how to do it. Quite irrespective of what appears to our human vision in terms of healing, something has to happen when we become exposed to God's perfection.

It seems that sometimes healing takes place instantaneously physically or mentally, and quite often it unfolds as a progressive experience. For example, one often finds that perhaps months later one meets an entirely new, vigorous, transformed personality, and that the healing took place step by step as some deep and searing situations became redeemed, released, forgiven.

Does The Healing Process Differ For Different Problems, Such As Mental Illness, Deformities, Viruses, Arthritis, Cancer, Etc.?

In human consciousness one does indeed become aware of the differing degrees of illness in mind or body or circumstance. We recognize the pain. We are given definition of cancer, arthritis, or whatever. We even through psychological and medical processes have some understanding, or belief, that there are indeed these various degrees of sickness from functional illness to organic disease.

For my part, conceiving as I do the absolute perfection of God, the almighty power of the spirit, I cannot accept that there could be any kind of human situation which could not be transformed by the Father.

Perhaps it is we, on the human level, who created an obstacle in that we recognize, believe, and accept that some things are more difficult to heal than others. For example, we have no difficulty in believing that a cut finger will automatically heal itself. It is easy to believe that prayer might heal a headache, give us peace of mind, take a pain away on some relatively trivial level. It is more difficult, perhaps, for most of us to conceive that God's instantaneous perfection can dissolve a cancer, or cure arthritis or some great deformity.

I find no difficulty in merging functional illness with organic disease. They are all part of the same system, and I believe are all equally open to the healing power to the degree we can accept it and motivate it. I think it is also true that very much organic disease is also the outward form of deep inward tensions and pressures. Not always, but in very many cases this has proved to be so. I think we should be wise always to contemplate the value of spiritual counselling linked with prayer, and the recognition of God's power to accomplish everything.

For instance, I remember one Sunday morning many years ago a lady came to the Sanctuary in a terrible state of mind. She told me that on the following Wednesday she had to go to the hospital to have her breast removed. She was really terrified. I talked to her, counselled with her, described the way God would be with the doctors and nurses and help her in every wonderful way to come out of this experience healed and blessed.

She made me feel her breast. It was like one great hard lump. As I talked and counselled, her fears subsided. Eventually I said we should now begin our prayer. I stood behind her, put my hands on her head, and thanked the Father for His wondrous presence. After two or three minutes in the silence, she suddenly exclaimed, "I'm healed!" She said she felt a pain in her breast and just knew everything had gone right. And so it was. She went to the hospital the following Wednesday, and the doctors could not relate the medical report with the present condition. She had been instantly healed.

I mention this particular case because it so happened that I met this lady about once each year for many years as I took Divine Healing Services in her town.

She always came to the meetings and she never had any more difficulty in her breast after those few moments in the quietness in the Sanctuary in prayer.

Are There Any Limitations To The Healing Process?

This is really answered in the various aspects of healing which are the theme of this writing. In God there can be no limitations. Even so we must realize the constancy of the human limitation and the degree in which we can accept the divine answer.

Why Are Not All People Healed At A Healing Session?

This, of course, has always been a great problem in the field of divine healing. It is certainly true in the experience of all healing ministries that some people are instantly healed, some are progressively healed, and some, indeed, are not physically healed at all. This certainly is a great grief to all of us, and I do not suggest for a minute that anyone really knows the complete answer to this particular problem. One can only suggest various aspects of the situation and comment on those.

I am sure one of the most urgent factors we must help

each other to understand and embrace is that we are spirits functioning in consciousness. As is very natural, a tremendous emphasis is always placed upon the physical sickness and, therefore, from a healing point of view there is equally tremendous concentration on healing the physical sickness itself. Far too little attention is given to the healing of the person. I would not wish to be glib about this in any sense of the word. I only know that it is true that so many difficulties of disease or disaster which one meets when someone comes asking for help and healing are the end-product of a long chain of discords, pressures, tensions of one kind or another. But not always, by any means.

I know it is not easy, even in good counselling, to uncover many of these causes. Sometimes they stretch right back to childhood experience. Sometimes there has been a great grief, a tremendous frustration, a deep period of anxiety which flows into the physical system as discord or disease. These inner turbulences may very well have taken place years ago and only now be coming out into manifestation.

Beyond this, of course, is a whole area in which the physical system is really preparing to release the spirit into the new life beyond this world. It would seem that in such cases all the divine healing one tried to implement would not heal the sick body. The true healing might well be the release of the spirit into heaven. When the natural time comes for departure, then we shall indeed all depart.

There is another acute factor to take into consideration. When any person has had a serious illness like arthritis, heart trouble, or cancer, which often becomes a deep and searing experience stretching into years, the pattern of the sickness is very deeply embedded in that person's life. To live with some of these terrible conditions induces a great fixation in the mind. And, it would seem, the gravity of the situation, the pain of it, is often so great that even prayer cannot make a break-through into the consciousness of the person concerned. Yet, I also know that God's love would be yearning to heal the situation. These are the problems which can only yield to much more experience in the work by many more people. Even Jesus found he could do no great works in His own area where people could not be inspired or lifted up to accept that the carpenter could do any works like that.

We do not really know the full measure of why people are not healed. On the other hand, and I think this is very significant, it is a common denominator experience of all who minister or people who have been involved in healing ministries that whenever prayer is made, something wonderful happens. There is always an action in the person for whom one prays which gives perhaps more courage, confidence, hope, or a feeling of being helped. The common denominator experience is that everyone is helped in some way. I would imagine, each person is helped by the Father to the degree that each needs or can accept at that particular time. I do not think it should ever be a question of despair or disillusionment on the part of the church, the prayer group, or the individual healer. Just as we do not close down our hospitals because some people die in them, neither should we suffer from limitation because some people are not healed.

I had to learn this lesson myself. I was very distressed in the early days because some people were favored with healing and others apparently not. It was then that I realized that my function was not to heal anyone, but rather to continue to be a channel of God's love and effectiveness into the life of the person for whom I prayed. It was His will that had to be done. Only the Lord could know what to do and how to do it. My function was to pray, to love, to do my very best to be an empty channel through which God's blessing could shine.

From then on my purpose could only be to continue to give thanks for His perfection shining in that person's life and to release that soul into God's good care and keeping, knowing that another step had been taken forward in that friend's life.

Nevertheless, we should all keep in mind the glorious example of Jesus Christ. His recognition of the Father's Perfection and Presence, was so complete that all the reported miracles were the instantaneous healing of both cause and effect!

Is The Healing Treatment To Be Given Only Once To A Patient Or Must It Be Renewed?

I have a profound belief that once a patient has been prayed for, the Father could never forget that prayer. I would suggest that the Lord continues to minister to that person night and day without ceasing. Could we know the whole truth, and abide with faith in that truth, then we would indeed know that once we had been prayed for, that everything was working for our highest and eternal good in a consistent and unfolding way.

Nevertheless, it is also true that human nature is often helped by constant encouragement. I have found that many people move into progressive healing as they consistently write to us. This keeps a channel open. The patient is reminded of the continuance of God's action. Many people come to a Healing Sanctuary week by week and are encouraged and quickened in their faith so that they continue to be open and receptive to the healing love which is changing their lives.

Will The Healing Process Continue If The Healer Stops Treatment?

As above described, I truly believe the Father never forgets a prayer. He would always wish to continue to bless the person. The patient equally needs to know that it continues, for then, of course he or she will enter into meditation, into the practice of the presence of God, thankful always to be receptive to the perfection shining in his or her life in a continuous process. Hence, again, the need for adequate teaching to inspire and guide people in their thinking in this direction.

Can Reasons Be Given For The Failure Of A Treatment?

Many suggestions in connection with this question have already been answered in the previous thoughts, but I do think the intercessor, the minister, does have the responsibility of being as free as possible from any kind of uncertainty, lack of compassion, or even the idea of having human skills in this area of healing.

The more loving, the more simple, the more he accepts the idea of God shining through, the more the minister eliminates the idea of failure from his own consciousness.

Does The Healer Visualize The Illness And Then Visualize It As Cured, Or Does He Visualize A Perfect And Healthy Person From The Start?

I find it often helps to know what the person's trouble is. On the other hand I know that the healing function takes place to the degree one switches away from the condition to an acceptance of wholeness, or perfection. In this sense I do not drop into concern for the sickness itself. It is a simple truth that nobody is interested in the illness, not even the Father. Everyone, including Christ, can only be interested in the solution, in the answer, in the perfection. Therefore, in healing I switch as quickly as possible from a recognition of the sickness itself to an understanding and acceptance that God's love is shining through to produce the perfect and healthy person.

Is The Touch Of The Healers Hands Necessary? What Purpose Does It Serve?

The traditional way of healing is, of course, the laying-on-of-hands and there are many sacramental church methods for this. The laying-on-of-hands can be done as a healer is motivated, sometimes the hands on the head, sometimes allowing the hands to seek the location of the pain or trouble. I have seen many an arthritic knee cleansed as I held my hands on the knee and declared God's perfection to be there. I have often known discs in the spine to slip into position as I held my hands over that place.

In my own concept I would say the use of the hands in personal contact healing is merely that they are used as a kind of focusing device, for example in a knee, and it is at this point that God's healing perfection is shining. It is that kind of recognition, that centralizing of the divine action at that point, which seems to be helpful to both patient and healer.

On the other hand, some of the best of all healings take place at a distance. I often think that this is simply because the person living a hundred miles away or a thousand miles away knows that contact healing is not possible. Therefore, the whole attention is given to being receptive to the prayer which has been asked for in a Sanctuary. The patient then is much more likely to sit quiet, or to lie in bed at night, with his or her attention fixed entirely upon the presence and perfection of God. This is often the best of all ways of healing because it does indeed keep one from being concentrated on the personality of the healer and turns the mind to the true reality of the Christ.

In the wider vision one must concede that the spirit of God does not need anyone's hands to place it where it already is in the life stream of any person anywhere in heaven or earth. Nevertheless, the function of the healing intercessor is to be receptive to inspiration and to use every facility, from counselling to the laying-on-of-hands or praying, for people at a distance according to the situation which arises. Sometimes sacramental means are very useful indeed. Sometimes a visit to a hospital involves one in silent prayer. We have to flow easily with the spirit, and be as free as the wind of the spirit. Then the Father will direct His energies, His inspiration, His guidance, for the highest well-being of the patient through the channel He has chosen in the intercessor.

In this context one must also recognize the healing techniques and great human skills as expressed through the entire medical profession. The greatest error we can ever fall into is to isolate oneself from the whole field and concept of healing. The Father will and does work through *all* channels of compassion, and this includes doctors, psychiatrists, nurses, hospital staffs, and every other person or place where the object is to serve humanity.

Many great discoveries will be made when there is a clearer concept and understanding of the spiritual nature of man. Then we shall have a great partnership of minister (healer), doctor, and patient linked in healing intercession and divine action flowing through all these channels.

What Is The Role Of The Patient?

The patient is, of course, all-important in the sequence of divine healing because this is where the need is. The whole attention of the intercessor is dedicated to a living rapport, a glowing partnership in love, with the patient for the well-being of the patient in every possible way. That is why counselling, inspiration, friendship, fellowship together in a spiritual project become so important to the patient. The whole effort, from a human point of view as well as from a divine point of view, is to break the patient free from the inhibiting influence of the mental-emotional causes of any disease and, of course, from the disease itself.

The essential vision and teaching as revealed by Jesus Christ are absolutely in line with the patient's needs. That is to say, anyone who becomes totally committed to accepting and implementing the teachings and promises of Christ must inevitably be moving towards a higher and more idealistic plane of mental, spiritual, and material experience.

The attitude of love will always quicken prayer. The faith which is simple enough to believe in the absolute perfection of God obviously gets the mind of the patient out of the way and helps him to become receptive to the continuous movement of the spirit. Anything which can be done to quicken the patient's expectancy of healing is always a step in the right direction.

We discovered, for example, in all our research work that while love is central to healing, prayer and worship naturally open the channel through which God's spirit can flow. Hope that is engendered in a patient and the faith which is implemented are great factors in a person's attitude to life and to his or her problems.

In addition to this we discovered that there is what I call the "Law of Expectancy." I found, very early in my ministry, that when expectancy on a quickened and exciting level was introduced into the prayer stream, then miracles greatly increased. Job when he said, "The things that I fear, come upon me," was expressing the Law of Expectancy on a negative plane. He was literally drawing into his experience the things he feared and thereby they became part of his real experience in life. Equally, in prayer, it is no use going on expecting the illness to continue, the pain to persist, the disaster to be made greater. The whole function of prayer is to turn one's attention away from the disease or the dilemma and to contemplate the perfection of God as a living reality manifesting in one's life.

The one awful thing which prevents so much answered prayer is the uncertainty factor, the sense of inadequacy, the lack of belief that we have faith enough, and so on. Better to be bold and say, "Well, Father, I don't pretend to know very much about anything, but thank you that you know it all. Therefore, Lord, I do not have to tell you anything. My problem is given into your keeping, Father, and I just know that something wonderful is happening. From this moment I am expecting miracles to floodlight my life morning, noon and night. And all night long while I sleep, miracles will be pouring into my whole being and preparing me for another wonderful day."

Something like that, boldly, enthusiastically, vividly, and extravagantly expressed, linked with faith and expectation, opens the way to wondrous events. It is no use abiding in the Father for five minutes and then living the next five months outside the orbit of that divine activity.

We have to encourage the patient to have a consistent and exciting expectancy of the wondrous power of God shining into his or her life, morning, noon and night, week in and week out, month in and month out. Then the patient truly enters into a miraculous experience of the real miracle of life itself unfolding in partnership with the Lord.

In this sense it is the role of the patient. The patient, the healer, and everyone else is really adventuring in living and learning how to live adequately. We only know, in the light of modern research and experience, that everyone has the responsibility of discovering the great laws, the great spiritual laws, whereby life can be lived more fully, more wondrously and more idealistically.

We are really emerging out of darkness into light. The healers, in the very many ministries in the world today are the way-showers into a new generation in which people will eventually from cradle to grave know, feel and believe in prayer and in spiritual principles as being basic to the science of well-being and creative fulfillment.

Can the patient be benefited simply by his proximity to a healer without conscious volition on the part of the healer?

Yes, this very often happens. I suppose nearly everyone has had the experience of going into a sick room and the person who was ill reported feeling so much better after the visit. The minister who is uplifted in the spirit of God, who knows the feeling of love and compassion for everyone, is at all times a "light unto the world." It literally does mean that everyone is blessed because that person passes near.

Very often, for example, at a Divine Healing Service, people have reported healing as we shook hands at the door in parting. I am sure the Father initiates many wonderful events once a channel of love and faith are open for His use.

Can a patient at a distance and unaware of the healers efforts on his behalf be healed?

Yes, this is a very common occurrence. We have had hundreds of cases where someone has written in asking for help and healing for a husband, a son, a wife, or a friend with an instruction, "Please do not say anything about it." Time and again healing takes place. And we just know that the very best thing anyone can ever do for anyone else in trouble is to ask someone to pray for the person concerned. Prayer never hurt anyone. To enfold someone in love is not a trespass.

We should note in this context that, although one knows about the importance of cooperation of the patient, the need for conscious dedication, repentance, and the implementation of love, faith, prayer in his or her own right, it is still true that much good work can be done by others on behalf of people who do *not* know they are being helped and who perhaps would not welcome being introduced to divine healing in any case.

We should note well that someone did of course need to exercise love and faith and prayer in order to allow the Father to release His benefits in the direction requested.

Can unconscious people, babies, and animals be healed by the efforts of the healer?

Yes, children are particularly receptive to divine healing. So long as someone can invoke prayer and believe in answers, then miracles can indeed very often happen for children. The child has no resistance. It is already open and receptive to the movement of the spirit, once it is released through prayer.

I have found, personally, that many sick children have been healed when parents have in their turn been healed of fear or worry about the sick child. I think we have to be very careful indeed about human negative influence on unprotected children. Worry and pressure shining through the love-field of a mother can be disastrous for a child who is sick. The greatest healing potential for a child is, of course, the parents themselves. But they, like healers in the sense we describe them, are obligated to release the child to the Father and believe in God's perfection shining there. They have to exercise their faith, their love, their prayers, and their expectancy and behold the child filled with the power of the living Christ.

The same truth applies for unconscious people. There is no difference simply because they are unconscious. Their spirit is still alive in the spirit of God and prayer can be the very best antidote to their particular problem.

Animals, like children, are tremendously receptive to healing prayer. We get a constant stream of letters from people asking us to pray for their pets, and they so often tell us of wonderful results.

Can a scoffer be healed in spite of his refusal to take the healing seriously?

To some extent this falls into the same category as praying for people who are unaware of the healer's efforts. In addition, there is the other factor of potential resistance through his unbelief and perhaps even condemnation.

It is quite wonderful what tremendous results can be accomplished in this whole area of prayer for anyone, without any exception. All we really need to know is that, to the degree we release love in prayer, then something wonderful is set into motion in a person's life.

I think we have to reach far above the judgment aspect of it. The scoffer, the unbeliever, is only one among us all who is seeking to live adequately and has an equal right to the Father's love as anyone else in heaven or earth.

It means too, that if such a person is to one's awareness needing help, then this immediately obligates us to initiate that help on his behalf. This, in turn, involves us in getting people to pray for him, to love him, to help him in every possible way without necessarily preaching to him at all.

I learned this very early in my ministry. I remember one day receiving a letter from a lady in England asking if it would be any good praying for a young man friend of hers, John, who was dying of advanced tuberculosis in both lungs. According to medical decree he had about three months to live. She wrote, "He is not only an atheist, but a very arrogant atheist . . . No one dares even approach him in his need, or suggest the church or any aspect of Christ's teaching."

Would it do any good praying for him? In those very early days I had to find out about every step forward. I remember sitting down with the Father and really seeking the right answer. Then I felt absolutely inspired about it. It was then that I realized that to pray for someone does not necessarily mean "converting" him, challenging him, preaching to him, but that to love him and pray for him must be always right.

I wrote to this lady and suggested that this should be our procedure and invited her to write to me every week and let me know how it went. I asked her to establish a covenant of prayer with me so we could behold the perfection of Christ shining in this young man in a continuous sequence. She agreed to do this and we proceeded accordingly.

In the very first week there was no more blood in his sputum. Very shortly he put on several pounds in weight. In three months time he was completely healed of the disease. He still did not know that anyone was in prayer for him, and no one dared to mention it.

I suggested to this lady that something very wonderful had certainly been happening and that we had better just keep up a continuance of our recognition that God's love was shining upon him, like sunshine, in a constant stream of blessing. Week by week she would write to me and tell me of keeping her covenant but reporting no more change whatsoever.

Another three months went by. Then one day she wrote to say that she was going to marry John. I then thought that this should certainly quicken many things in their lives and indeed gave thanks to the father that wonderful things were certainly happening in those two people.

After another three months she reported no change whatsoever in the spiritual outlook. Then, one day about nine and a half months after the beginning of our intercessions, she told me how John had suddenly started talking about the miracles of Jesus Christ. She was astonished. Then she told him what had happened, how she had asked the Sanctuary to join in prayer for him, and how he had gotten well.

He turned to her and said with surprise, "Well, what else do you expect when you pray!" It seemed as though all the atheism, the uncertainty, had just automatically disappeared. It was as though after all those months the healing love of God just shone through in his consciousness.

They became members of a prayer group. Interestingly enough I began with the physical healing and ended up with true spiritual healing.

I have a very great feeling and concern for this entire area of experience. So many human situations like family discords could be easily healed if people would only become involved in *patient, silent* prayer for the husband, the wife, the son, or the daughter.

Too often, in our weak human nature, we so easily fall into judgment and condemnation of the one who "goes off the rails," who is in a state of discord. How wonderful if, instead of trying to preach or force transformation, we could silently but lovingly, behold the perfection of God shining in the one for whom we have concern. Inevitably, then, divine transformations tend to unfold in the life and personality for his or her highest and eternal good. Loved ones in the midst of the scene are often the most important factors for such a transformation. Love is the only channel which can make that kind of healing possibility come true.

What a challenge this is to family members because, after all, our lives are centered in the family unit and it is at *this* very point that we must find our highest and our best in expression.

What is the most cooperative and ideal behavior on the part of the patient?

In the end, beyond the pains, the sicknesses, the loneliness, and all the afflictions of man, must inevitably lie the great love factor that is the central flame of life itself. We all know about this love. We all recognize the need for being loved. When love flies out of our lives we are indeed out on a desert without water, marching in an arctic waste, or lost in the darkness.

What is not always so clearly understood is that love, even in healing, has very little to do with what we can *get* from God or from people. It has very much to do with what we can give, and give, and give to the Father, to the world, to our social structure, to our families and, indeed, to our daily work.

Loving has to do with giving, not getting. So many miracles of healing take place when we turn our attention away from ourselves and seek an objective for living joyously so that others may be prospered and blessed because we pass their way.

In the end, the Christ way is, indeed, a perfect pattern for everyone to follow, and this not only opens the way to personal healing but is the sure way whereby we can be channels of effective and infinite and multiplying good to everyone whose lives touch ours. That, surely, is the basic purpose of life itself because it leads, inevitably and in the long term, to the fulfillment of God's will upon earth, the establishment of His Kingdom of Love, the establishment of the brotherhood of man in the Fatherhood of God on earth, as it is in heaven.

Mama Mona Ndzekeli

Biographical Sketch

Mama Mona is President of the African Spiritual Church in South Africa. Her deep compassion and the accuracy of her messages have produced thousands of well-documented healings and psychic messages. Through her understanding of the ancestral background of her people, she has followed the tribal customs and blended them with her own high order of Christianity. Mama Mona has become a spiritual force.

We last saw Mama Mona in Manhattan where she had come from Africa to a healing session. She was accompanied by her husband, a fine, erudite man who is deeply involved with her work. He is the pastor of her Spiritualist Church.

Mama Mona, a beautiful woman whose face expresses her high ideals of service and love, does not speak English, so our conversation was interpreted back and forth by her pleasant and intelligent assistant who sat beside her. Mama's luminous eyes were on our faces as we spoke, alert to the questions and anxieties we expressed as if she needed no interpreter but caught our questions on the conduits of the mind. She sat quietly, wrapped in a powerful stillness, her white robes hanging in biblical folds.

At one of her sessions, when asked to hurry with individual hearings because time was getting short, she replied through her interpreter, a definite no. She said, "The spirit guides who are here must be given time to finish each individual completely, or they will not be available." No further effort was made to hurry Mama Mona.

At one point in the session we saw her pause a moment in her healing activities as if listening for something. The room was silent but Mama rose to her feet. We followed her gaze and saw a young woman in the audience crying soundlessly. Mama asked her interpreter and patient to wait. She walked down the aisle in her long white robe and lifting one edge of her flowing veil, covered the young weeping woman's face and head. Mama said a few words, waited a minute or two and removed the veil. The young woman who had been so distressed was now smiling and radiant, revealing the strong inner reassurance given by Mama. Mama Mona returned to her place on the dais as if this were just an ordinary happening.

Mama Mona's handshake as she completes her healing and says goodby is her own unique way of conveying reassurance and energy. Current passed between us as she held each hand in one of hers.

Following are her own words about her background.

*   *   *   *   *

As I consider my life, it becomes clear to me that I was born to serve. On the day I was to be born, May 24th in 1922, my mother was ducking bullets from an angry crowd of European strikers. It was an all-white mine strike for higher wages. My mother struggled to a nearby township about ten miles from the center of Johannesburg in the Transvaal. As soon as I was born, we were taken to a deserted mine shaft to be safe until all was clear and the strike was over. My mother recalled with horror the prevalence of rats and insects down there.

As I grew up, I heard many stories, often spoken in Zulu, of my parents' past experiences. The stories interested me. I was a shy and lonely child and I had begun to realize that I was different in some way and did not meld with the company of other children.

At school I surprised my teachers because learning

anything was no problem. The words that came from the teacher were engraved in my mind sometimes before she spoke them. I led the class until spinal meningitis and a long convalescence cut off my formal education.

It is clear to me now that I was a born psychic. From early childhood I had many visions. A familiar and recurrent one surrounded me with very small babies with wings. I flew with them in what I know was the spirit world. I would love to hear the music now that I heard then in the spirit world, sounds of a soul-penetrating sweetness to which every cell in my person vibrated in harmony. As a child I felt a naive wonder that the world did not encourage me to report these marvels.

One day I went on a spirit journey with a guide who took me through rocks and streams with ease, as if matter was no barrier. We went through a mountain and saw mystical things, which I was warned not to speak of and never will. From that time on, my psychic powers matured. I wondered at the people around me who lived their daily lives with no clue to the existence of all these realities in other dimensions.

From time to time the guide, who had taken me on the journey to the core of the mountain, would speak to me, coming clearly through my everyday life, bringing me messages from the time dimension such as, "That man you are talking to is only going to live for seven days." I would pray hard for that man's easy departure and his progress through the spirit world.

Even though these communications from the spirit world were known, people still considered me only a dreamer, and it was not until my prophecies were reported as true that I became respected as a psychic.

I cannot really make an accurate account of my powers. In other words, some of the things I do are just as mysterious to me as they are to you.

When I grew up and became a young married woman, many people would come to me to ask me to solve their problems. I could not understand this—I was so young in worldly experience. However, I felt a love for these people, good or bad, dull or sprightly, and let them all come to drink tea with me in my garden. Most of my guidance comes in messages as I tend my flowers. These messages are never vague but always precise and clear.

As I laughed and chatted with my friends and listened to their difficulties, their problems both mental and physical, seemed to melt away instantaneously or shortly afterward. In this way I gradually became aware that I had the healing gift. My friends began sending their children to me to be healed, and through the grace of my spirit guides, they were healed.

My babies were shown to me before they were born, and I was able to inform my husband of their sex and characteristics at the beginning of each pregnancy. When I had had enough children, one of the guides sent some spirit midwives, one of whom touched my womb. I could feel this and knew that, from then on, I would have no more children. I was meant to channel my energies elsewhere.

When I became an active member of the Methodist Church and enrolled in the women's guild, I studied and tried to understand the light-filled dimensions of Christ. At this time my spirit guides instructed me that the power of prayer was essential for spiritual development, not only the prayer for the well-being of others but for my own development. I must pray specifically for that. There must be an active thrust of the human spirit towards its own development, as a strong plant grows toward the light and opens its petals.

Pray, ask for accurate guidance, then listen inwardly, and keep on listening until finally you hear. If I had depended on the prayers of others for my own development, I would not have now the spiritual authority to heal, nor would I have founded my healing center and trained my capable healing probationers.

When I became a member of the Healing Association of Africa, I started my official healing. Africa is fraught with magic, and some of my healing is done on cases of witchcraft. Unfortunately with many Africans, witchcraft is practiced both seriously and just for sport, to see what the human will can do. I do not like to take magic cases or to be called a magician.

When people come to my husband and say that they have lost hope and ask for a sitting with his wife, he usually says, "If you have lost hope, who is going to find it for you? Search for it and take it to Mama Mona." He knows that out of compassion I will not turn such hopeless people away. However there are some people that I do refuse to treat, those who ask for witch's water. I know these people are skeptical and will run back to the witch doctor to complete the treatment. I, therefore, pray for the progression of their spirits, and send them away.

There are certain African ritualistic ceremonies that are considered important in order to relate to our tribal ancestors. I have often met my great-grandfather, Mhlonhlo, in the spirit world. He was a renowned psychic in his day and because I have been in communication with him I am considered a foremost healer.

Because important rituals enable me to reach more of my people, I determined to take certain of my healing center probationers with me to a famous river where ritual baths are performed. The river was infested with dangerous crocodiles and other lethal inhabitants. If the mediums are pulled under and devoured by the crocodiles, then they are considered unclean spiritually and should not have entered the waters. I was certain that the ceremony would pass over smoothly for us, and it did. All mediums of importance must undergo this ceremonial ritual for strengthening and for the medium's future success with the African tribes.

Sometimes I will go to a house where there is much trouble. I never enter any house or gathering without a strong prayer for harmony within, a practice I recommend to everyone. I do believe that I must take what is given to me to do as a prophet and a healer by the grace of my light-filled guides.

MAMA MONA SPEAKS

*(The following was taped by Mama
Mona's husband, Reverend Ndzekeli.)*

Following is a statement on behalf of my wife, Mama
Mona Ndzekeli. It is a series of talks including the
answering of questions in response to your request.

I'll start with an introductory reading and an explanation, which might lead to a better understanding of what
African spiritualism is and what contributions we can
make to this book.

First, the word miracle which is defined in the introduction to this book. That word in our own African
language is *Esimangalisayo*. There is no excitement
among the African races regarding this phenomena.
African life abounds with miracles. The Western races
have long considered Africa as being superstitious, since a
miracle has no real scientific explanation or proof. But
miracles have always been accepted by Africans without
question or test.

A number of miracles occurred to Mama Mona's
ancestors. Her great great-grandfather was Chief
Mhlonhlo of the Mpondomise tribe, a dynasty of chiefs
who loved fighting. He was also a psychic. During the
time of the early settlers in the Cape, unsuccessful at-
tempts were made to capture him. On one occasion his
enemies approached his hiding place, and when a bullet
was fired, a dense fog descended which slowed the settlers advance and caused them to shoot one another instead of Chief in their confusion.

In Mama Mona's home district, she has often been surrounded with a visible portion of fog that descends on her alone. People with whom she walks after dusk have experienced this and understood the cause, knowing Mama Mona's family background. We have heard footsteps in the fog, walking beside her, footsteps of guides who sing and talk to her.

We have been accused by our African ancestors as being a generation that is fast deteriorating morally because we have gone away from our gods who once spoke to us. The gods have now renounced any contact with the modern generation because of our cynicism. Listen to this one. "If you have powers granted by the gods and consider yourself a son of God, let's see you turn these stones into food." The older tribal Africans, however, are still deeply imbued with the religion and ways of their ancestors, and this mystical current flows through the subconscious minds of all Africans, young and old.

Another line in the introduction of this book is "Mental Universe." Yes, most Africans would endorse this definition. Actually the African has never really believed that he lives one active life only. He always says, "After each step, I have visited with the gods and with so and so," naming people in the spirit world or far away. By "after each step" he means after each sojourn here on earth. He might then relate a conversation with spirits in which a suggestion was given to help someone, perhaps a barren woman who desires children. The spirits may order a beast to be slaughtered in order that a symbolic ceremony be performed. This barren woman would always bear a child, a baby from the spirit world.

There are many ways of modern healing, such as mentioned in the preface written by the compilers—hypnotic treatment, contact healing with the magnetic touch, and so on. All these methods may or may not bring instantaneous healing.

The modern Africans are just beginning to emerge

from the healing powers of the witch doctor, whose skill depended upon herbs and a direct line to their ancestors. There is not much deliberate hypnotic healing among the Africans. Most of their healing lies in the power of the words in a healing ceremony and in contact healing. All sickness, according to African tribal belief, is caused by ceremony conducted wrongly or not conducted at all, to the wrath of the ancestors.

In some cases, a very sick man, almost dying, would be taken to the cattle kraal and be dumped in there among the animals. The psychic healer would call all the next of kin to come and create power to heal the sick man. The participants must go through a cleansing or purifying ceremony in order to be suitable to ask the ancestors' forgiveness on behalf of the sick, and they must be pure themselves. The words would go something like this: "Son of so-and-so, great-grandson of so-and-so, we have brought you here before this holy place in the cattle kraal. May the great ancestors heal you instantly." After these words, the cattle in the kraal must pass their water as a sign to indicate that the plea has been answered and that the healing has been achieved.

This seems ridiculous, but to this day many of the tribes believe that healing takes place in the cattle kraal. As seen from the eyes of the African, the kraal was not only the commercial power of the African people but it was also their center of interest. This is where all the ancestors of the family would be buried.

However, when those who will, and they are legion, come to Mama Mona in her Spiritual Church, she performs wonders for them in contact healing and absent healing. She also exorcises evil spirits.

In some of Mama's work she has received assistance from several relatives who have died. This has surprised us both since some of these relatives would never have been expected to help anybody.

In many of Mama Mona's healings, a guide, a Sister Superior, sends messages that never miss the mark. It is unbelievable but true. The guide performs marvels and gives simple instructions which are passed on by Mama Mona according to the spiritual and cultural level of the patient. Because of this they can be easily understood and carried out.

For example, somebody came to Mama Mona with a terrible illness. Mama, guided by the invisible Sister Superior, sent one of her grandchildren to "fetch water from the tap and give it to her to drink." The patient was healed instantaneously. To another patient, she said, "Just say, 'Our Father Which Art In Heaven,' and repeat it seven times, and then the sickness will come out." Then we would have a report in the morning that there had been an instantaneous healing after the prayer had been said seven times. Another time, she said, "Buy a handkerchief and bring it here so that I can bless it, then send it to your ailing aunt." The woman would be healed when she received the handkerchief.

Another method of absent healing would be to tell somebody to buy tobacco and get somebody to just puff the smoke saying, "I am smoking this on behalf of so-and-so who is already in spirit." This smoking by somebody in the spirit world on behalf of a sick person enables the sick one to come out of the house completely cured. Another time Mama Mona might say, "Let me pat you three times on the back," and the pain would be gone immediately. To another, "Buy yourself a blue cape, I'll bless it. Wear it when you go to prayer meetings or church and you will be healed." Color plays an important part in Mama's healing.

Now that you have become acquainted with Mama Mona, we will go on to the questions.

What is the primary source of the healing power?

The primary source of all healing power is God. In creation God used the power of thought.

The ancestors of our African people believed in the full power of prayer. The most important step to take when you are included in a community is that of going to the high mountain to pray for rain, preceded, of course, by purity and fasting. This was always necessary before the prayer ceremony. Just before the people descended from the mountain, the rains would always fall down. Never once has this prayer not been answered here in our area. We modern Christians have tried this without success and the drought becomes more intensive. We have been accused, therefore, of having no power over the elements.

The primary source of healing other people is the spirit power of the individual. Mama Mona tells would-be healers, "You must be in strength to heal any disease and healing should be instant."

African healing has always been accompanied by wonderful singing to raise the power. Patients have been watched reacting to Mama's healing with jerks and sparks as the result of electric shocks. Some have recorded electric shocks when touched through her contact healing.

Why is a human channel necessary to contact the healing power?

The spirit guides come through under such conditions as I have mentioned, and of course human channels are necessary because the guides work through the instrumentality of the healer. Remember how Christ said that he would give his feet, hands, and power to his disciples to further the mission, which was healing, preaching and teaching.

What is the difference between magnetic and spiritual and faith healing?

I have explained magnetic above, and now I will add that Mama Mona does not shake hands. This is a very controversial issue that sometimes embarrasses her here when she must refuse to shake hands. She has magnetic healing powers and every time she shakes hands—by that I mean when she is not doing it for the purpose of healing—her powers are expended or wasted because the handshake would leave her sensitive hands feeling numb and sick. A lot of her healing has been done by a special handshake. At that time her clothes have been seen to shower electric sparks. The handshake has also been used in her healing center in the development of healers. On this subject many African witch doctors also refuse handshakes, saying that this draws their power.

Spiritual healing to us Africans is the intervention by the spirit guides who prescribe the method of healing to be used. For example, a young boy came to our center to be healed of a gangrenous toe. He had been taken from one doctor to another, from one hospital to another, without finding any help. Somebody suggested Mama Mona Ndzekeli, the Moroka Prophet, as she is called. The sick boy was accompanied by relatives. This is very typical of African affairs, a deputation always. The boy had a sitting with Mama Mona in which the boy's dead grandfather came through. He spoke to the medium, Mama Mona, and told her to tell his wife, the boy's grandmother, to send this boy to a circumcision ceremony. They did, and with the healing of the circumcision operation, the boy was healed. This is just one example of the many such spiritual healings which were always suited to the understanding of the patient.

Mona always says that a non-cooperative or non-believing patient can be saved in spite of himself in spiritual healing but not in faith healing. In faith healing, he is saved by himself via his own belief. Christ said, "Your faith has saved you and has made you whole." In faith healing you are saved by faith and by grace even though the grace may be undeserved. This type of healing is usually done at secret prayer meetings run by faith healers. Mediums do not fit in squarely with faith healing. In most cases they are not desired or needed.

Are these gifts mutually exclusive or can the healer use any method at will?

I will say that a healer cannot use these at will. Only a medium or a psychic can use any method. The rest of the healing people can not deviate from their accustomed procedure.

Can anyone be a healer?

Yes, it seems that this gift is common among the African people. Many Africans who were never interested in spiritualism or related activities have died and become impressive healing guides. Many African families have their family collections of these deceased relatives whose intelligence they have access to and whose healing is available to them. This has resulted in a great deal of spiritual healing. To most Africans spiritualism is a fashion and one who is not a prophet is looked down upon. In fact, some call those not committable to spiritualism, ghouls.

Dedication is a method by which any one of us can improve our psychic powers. "Ask and ye shall be given, look and it shall be open to you."

What qualities are needed to become a channel for healing?

You will excuse me if I use African standards in answering most of these questions. It will make a wonderful variation. I am also using Mona's standard, love (L-O-V-E) conquers all. She has always warned the healers she trains against their own tempers and dark moods that hang on and on. She says, "Do not go to bed before cleansing your consciousness, particularly the centering of your spirit. Only thereafter can you relax and meditate, and the spirit of God just pours into you.

This quality of love will open the way to becoming a healing channel. If we could all radiate love, we could cure all the ills of this century. Love God, love your neighbor, and radiate love to others. Remember, the things you do to other people, good or bad, are returned to you a thousand fold."

I wish I had time to tell you of all the good my wife Mama Mona has done a thousandfold.

Is it necessary to make a diagnosis? If so, how is it done?

It is not really essential to diagnose a patient, although it may help to give a skeptic confidence if he realizes that the healer knows what is wrong with him. Mama Mona herself does not really care for such diagnosis. She always interests herself in finding the real cause. She leaves diagnosis to the healer probationers working under her, just to give them training.

There are so many symptoms that come to her healing sanctuary, terrible headaches that persist, diseases of the chest that may be tubercular, and ailments that seem incurable, such as leprosy and related diseases. Mama Mona does not linger over the symptoms. She goes directly into the cure. African mediums go into trances very easily, light trances in which they are free to laugh and joke.

Does unusual heat emanate from the hands of the healer?

The answer is yes, it does. Some patients have acknowledged this feeling on a number of occasions. In fact, the more a healer gives out heat, the more water he needs to drink.

Do healers project an invisible healing light?

Yes, healers do project a light, the quality of which depends upon the giver. Mama Mona has seen and described balls of fire falling upon the heads of the persons being helped, even upon her own head.

Sometimes apprentice healers have been given authority in our Spiritualist Churches to just stay and do what the spirit requires of them to do for any person. This can be abused if the amateur healers try to show off and steal the show.

Is a healer tired or refreshed after a healing?

The healer is definitely refreshed and renewed. Once a message has been given or carried out, it is a wonderful refresher for the healer who sits down and calls on the saints. There have been some cases, however, when Mama Mona had to retire and rest. This is when evil spirits have been exorcised by her.

Nearly all African tribes recognize witchcraft. I am sorry to say this. There are of course a few exceptions. I think when the Africans emerge from that stage where survival is for the fittest, then all will be well.

Does the healer consciously raise his vibrations and generate psychic energy?

As I have said, Africans raise their vibrations and power by singing and dancing, with or without the accompaniment of drums and clapping of hands, in almost jazz rhythms and tunes. You could call in any modern popular musician or composer, and he would have no trouble following us and could find new inspiration as the energies and vibrations rise. When the music reaches its peak, the spirit guides come in abundance.

It is considered a disgrace among Africans to be unable to sing with harmony of voice. Mama Mona often accuses me of bad singing and she has not allowed me to start chanting. She always tells me, as a joke in the family, that I put her off by my singing and my poor ear. I sit far away from her so that she cannot trace my bad notes. She has a wonderful musical ear and she comes from a family of musicians. A developed medium is always conscious of sound vibrations.

Does the healer connect with a healing guide? A pool of cosmic wisdom? Or achieve oneness through prayer?

A healer connects with a healing guide. The power of prayer is most important. If Mama Mona did not have great powers of prayer, I doubt if so many successful healings could have been achieved.

What is the healing process?

I have seen Mama Mona treat the same conditions differently. Mental illnesses are dark illnesses, and yet such diseases of the mind are cured in our church by Mama Mona and her helpers.

The tribes that use witchcraft believe that the evil spirits are collected from the areas near the graves of various nationalities, which explains to them why their possessed ones can sometimes speak more than four languages.

Does the healing process differ for different problems such as mental illness, deformities, viruses, arthritis, cancer, etc.?

Mama Mona can heal these troubled cases by exorcising them in the name of Christ who casts out all demons.

In some African tribes it is suspected that the deformity of a child is a curse or punishment visited upon the parent. It is not God's creation, they argue, but Mama replies that everything is God's creation. We each have our challenges and their purpose must be discovered. When this is done, it is often simultaneous with the cure.

I have made a thorough study of hospitalization in Africa. Lots of serious diseases are treated in hospitals, but I have discovered that more patients go to hospitals and doctors just to obtain a legal document for being absent from work or for a death certificate. In case of death, evidence must be shown before burial or a post mortem is performed, which is hated by all Africans.

Are there any limitations on the healing process?

Only death, and once it is realized that this is inevitable, as is often the case, then the path of the spirit in the new world must be prepared by instructing the person as to the conditions he must expect when he passes over.

Why are not all people healed at a healing session?

All are not healed for the following reasons. Some mediums will work at a break-neck pace, and this is not conducive to good healing. Many people come only to take a chance and really don't believe what goes on, and this lowers the vibrations. They are not in accord with the healer. The power of thought is important when people are assembled for the occasion, and many of them do not fully believe in the power of healing at the same time.

Can reasons be given for the failure of a treatment?

Mama Mona was asked why a baby was born blind and what sin he had committed to bring upon him this catastrophe. She quoted Christ when he said that God reveals himself to man in more than one way, in order to teach him.

Is the healing treatment to be given to a patient only once or must it be renewed?

It is advisable for the patient to stay and be checked. It is also important for a patient to be advised and seen again, for he must not go back to the conditions that made him sick. In Mama Mona's sanctuary, special days are set aside for this.

Will the healing process continue if the healer stops treatment?

Yes, the healer visualizes the continuation of the cure, and healing continues. The guides have already told the healer how well the patient will be if the treatment were performed on him, and the healer holds this picture.

Is the touch of the healer's hands necessary? What purpose will it perform?

It is necessary for conductivity to the success of some cases. The tender touch of a loving healer can cause great changes in a patient by giving comfort and energy, and then the patient becomes more cooperative.

What is the role of the patient?

In the reported sensations of the patients, there are many emotional reactions. Some patients have wept bitterly after a healing. It is the shock of suddenly feeling wonderfully well. Others weep for the joy of new health and being told how his departed have helped him in this spiritual healing. For some time after the healing, the patient will reflect the light that comes from the healer who has been radiating health and love.

Can unconscious people, babies, and animals be healed by the efforts of a healer?

Yes, healers have often helped animals, in the same way as an unbeliever can be helped just by the spirit guide that does the healing. All animals, no matter how ferocious seeming, are actually very kind and love to be petted. They are comforted when someone is petting them, and this in itself carries a healing. The cure comes when they realize that the healer loves them and is doing this to remove whatever is causing their pain.

Can a scoffer be healed in spite of his refusal to take the healing effort seriously?

Yes. Mama Mona has even helped skeptics and scoffers. Some healers of a scoffer administer a cleanser drink and this is impressive to him. But the bitter taste of the cleanser may have no healing powers at all.

Mama Mona, however prefers Divine Water. Some people come from afar to ask Mama Mona for Divine Water. She politely refuses, saying, "I have not been guided to give you Divine Water. I'll give it to you if the guides so instruct me."

Many alcoholics have been helped, even some whose wives come without the husband to ask Mama for help.

They have been told to bring a shirt or trousers, jacket or shoes. As soon as these are placed before the healer, the guides have come through with remarkable messages and remedies that cure the alcoholics, as well as skeptics and scoffers and other similar patients.

What is the most cooperative and ideal behavior on the part of the patient?

Patients keeping appointments on time respond very well. Guides keep time, and when the time expires they go away. That is a difficulty we have had in the healing center. Guides have said, "Tell him to come at 9:00 A.M. tomorrow and we will have something for him." If the patient is not there, the guides hang on a few minutes, then leave. We have experienced our troubled moments in the center when the appointment has not been kept and the guides are unavailable to the medium.

Comments by Reverend Ndzekeli, Mama Mona's husband.

I would like to say a few words about the dangerous loss of our old knowledge with nothing but scientific know-how to replace it. If we could only combine the values of the old and the new.

Our old, instinctive knowledge is receding to the far past as our ancestors pass away. When I grew up as a small boy, stories of the wrath of the gods and of our ancestors were very common. The anger of our ancestors was due to their descendants not keeping to the divine laws as they understood them. My ancestor, who is now my spirit guide, used to tell me miraculous things that happened during our early days. Some of these he never saw, but the stories were brought down from generation to generation.

But man has fallen away from the gods except in a few cases. In the early days of Africa, the gods spoke to every man at any time without causing any comment and with no question as to the reality of their communications.

My great-grandfather told of some of the incredible operations that men of old performed, the amputation of hopeless limbs, with no pain and complete healing. In those days man lived with the wild beasts. My great-grandfather looked at me saying, "My child, even your face would be repulsive to the animals, your smell, your ways, and your whole appearance. You would be devoured. But we lived with the animals and they respected us." I asked why we can not live with the animals now. He said, "Man has fallen from his greatness and the beasts no longer have respect for him. Man has lost his status and is no longer worthy of trust. Man possessed endless knowledge, but when he deteriorated and was stripped of his rank, all of the qualities pertaining to this rank were also taken away from him, leaving him closed to the understanding of phenomena and revelation."

"Show us a sign." This question is often asked of the spirits by those who deal with the world beyond. They know that the public wants proof of what they say.

One day I remarked to a blind friend that it was cloudy and overcast and might rain in a moment. Indeed the humidity was such that one could take off his jacket, very typical of African weather. My friend said, "This is unbelievable with so much heat. I can feel the rays of the sun and I just love it." Later he said, "Anyway, my friend, what do I see and why should I argue? But what do any of us see, really, to argue against those who have a third eye when we have only two?" It is a very reasonable question to ask.

Now coming to materializations, they are very common things. Nobody gets excited over these phenomena in Africa. Head boys would report messages from their departed grandparents with whom they had been conversing at the pastures while they were looking after the cattle. The messages were received without prejudice.

Africans, being familiar with strange experience, can tell you if the spirit they have encountered has strength. They believe that if a spirit is weak and stranded, it is because the spirit has not been received at the other end. They relieve the spirit by a simple ceremony to the ancestor.

Occasionally someone who has died but has not yet left his earthly path is bewildered and confused. He speaks in a rambling way and appears a fool to a living relative. However, his message is taken without prejudice. Such problems are settled by asking the spirit of the departed to go and rest in peace in his own way. Help is asked from the guides, and this is achieved for him.

The subject of reincarnation in the Western world is a burning subject. There are scientific experiments, and mediums are toiling sweat and blood to try to convince the skeptics of this truth of spiritual being and phenomena. They do seem to be getting somewhere. In African life, however, we have not had that trouble, not at all. Reincarnation is a foregone conclusion. No records are kept here, but a newborn child is known because the spirit has announced its own coming back. For instance, a departed relative or friend announces that he or she will be born to so-and-so's daughter. Sometimes an unknown spirit is announced, and he or she will be met and welcomed.

We may not have such records as other people keep, of materializations and other phenomena, because these subjects are so common here that there is no need to question or tabulate them.

I have always said that we should combine our efforts to prove to the world the higher realities of spiritualism and that a probe of African life would greatly reward the research. I believe that the missing link to a higher reality is here. This is the perfect practicing ground if only the western world would come here to study Africa, the cradle of spiritualism.

Some people have called African spiritualism just superstition, but it is gaining acceptance now all over the world that the Africans had a reason to believe that there was no death and that you only pass through a veil. We say if you have left your old suit, you will get a new suit in the new world.

Friends, on behalf of Mama Mona Ndzekeli of the African Spiritualist Church, we thank you and are very grateful that this information reaches you. Rest assured that all the information that I have given you is direct from Mama Mona.

Oh Shinnah

Biographical Sketch

Oh Shinnah can truly be called one of our American resources. Her experience spans a broad spectrum of cultures, grounded equally in the ancient traditions of The People of Turtle Island (the ancient name for the Americas) and in the contemporary reality defined by modern research and teaching.

Her initial learning came from her father, a full-blooded Apache who speaks fourteen languages, and her great-grandmother, a Mohawk and a Theosophist, both of whom did healing. Oh Shinnah's mother was of Mohawk and Scotch descent. As an adult she became the "adopted" daughter of Rolling Thunder, the famous healer.

Oh Shinnah knows well the natural ways of healing and ceremony. She has studied ancient cultures and knows all the ways of herbal healing. She has herself a harmonious relation with nature and all her creations, including the use of gems and crystals in healing.

To this strong base of ancient knowledge from her heritage, she has added her own intellectual attainments in modern psychology. She holds a master's degree in experimental psychology and is very much in contact with the latest medical practices. This combination provides a powerful and very intelligent use of healing energy.

One of Oh Shinnah's goals is to bring to the public an awareness of self-healing. In her workshops and lectures she shows us the way to heal ourselves with the use of spiritual energy, crystals and self-knowledge. To combine spiritual and physical healing is one of the themes of her teachings.

Our strongest impression of Oh Shinnah is one of harmony. We feel her friendliness with the earth itself and somehow we are certain that there is a reciprocal friendship coming to her from the earth, trees and water. Her radiant face and the clear intelligence of her eyes holds us and we feel stronger, deep inside. We are in harmony with her and with her beloved earth. If there were more such healing forces as Oh Shinnah, the planet earth would be in less danger from the near-fatal side effects of our careless and ruthless treatment.

Oh Shinnah's work with crystals is especially interesting to us for we had always kept crystals about the house for their depth, beauty and mysterious strength. A friend showed us how holding a block of crystal in one hand strengthens the other empty hand. If the tip of the thumb and forefinger are held together against the effort of another person to separate them, the crystal will mysteriously add strength and resistance, but without the crystal held in the other hand, the fingers of the empty hand open easily. We are enthralled by Oh Shinnah's work with crystals in healing. Using the natural gem formation of the earth in pure form to communicate the healing strength of the earth seems a most natural process.

Oh Shinnah has taken her special wisdom, insight and experience all over the country and abroad in seminars and workshops. She has also attended the United Nations Conference on Ecology, Stockholm, Sweden; the World Conference of Spiritual Leaders, New York; and the United Nations Conference on Racism and Decolonization of Indigenous People, Geneva, Switzerland.

She has brought many people to spiritual awareness and also to a realization of the plight and value of our most precious asset, the very earth that sustains us and is now being defaced and brutalized. Oh Shinnah is a friend of the earth and of the people on it and spends her days and herself in striving to cure and sustain both.

OH SHINNAH SPEAKS

Illuminated,
the spark of my essence took fire,
casting light
upon the shadows
of all remembrances,
consuming rage and regret.

Like comets blazing star paths
across deep midnight skies,
my soul raced outward,
seeking solace
from its weary journey
through Life's indifferences.
Touching and fusing
with forces beyond comprehension,
my being exploded
into a
thousand million particles,
blended with the fabric of
All Glorious Creation,
forever surrendered, forever changed.

From the moment of my fusion with Source, personal history has had no importance with regard to what the truth is. For indeed, the truth is vibratory and requires nothing from the carrier, be it book or two-legged.

Let me introduce myself, Oh Shinnah, confrontation to fixed reality, infant beam in the light of Great Spirit's universes, citizen of earth, renegade.

This time of change and purification offers us a most unusual opportunity. By sharing our knowledges and ways, we may lose our fear of each other, and come to understand we share a common root. We are born alone, we die alone, there is but one Source, we have a common problem. The Earth is in famine, the waters and the children die, we walk the brink of war.

When the Great One reopens the doors of our true seeing and miracle becomes ordinary, it becomes obvious that there is but one work—to be a warrior of light—to go beyond personal, emotional prejudices and do what must be done to further the advance of Conscious Perfect Being.

My choice in this life has been to sing the songs of the Great Mother, following the path of nurturing and care, to cling to the beautiful dream, and work to help create a world free of malice.

What is the primary source of healing power?

All power is from above. Expressions of that power, whether for healing or evil, pure or perverted, are determined through the one who has found a path to the source of all power. The consciousness and heart of the one who seeks power is expressed in earthly terms in the work; i.e., to heal or to hinder.

There is something in me that says Source is nonjudgmental and good or evil a matter of free will, according to individual understandings. Therefore, the reflection of union with all there is will often result in the illusion referred to as miracle.

Why is a human channel necessary to conduct the healing power?

This is a difficult question to answer. The two-legged is so very arrogant in believing that healing is accomplished only through the human. The Water Spirits heal and require only the one in need of healing; no channel is necessary. The Tree Brothers and Sisters can free us of stress and pain. All we need do is put our feet naked upon the earth.

Root to root we stand
the trees and I
They, with their feet
reaching downward
rich, moist, warm soil.
Earth-bound are we.
One, with the desire
to be free
of the
confines of
Breath.

As humans, we channel the power of healing through an opening made by our love, compassion and surrender. We couple our energies with the forces of nature and spirit by becoming free of the attachment to being the doer, therefore becoming an integral part of the doing. *What is the difference between magnetic, spiritual and faith healing?*

Faith healing requires one's belief system, and is usually accomplished in a religious context, whereas magnetic and spiritual healing require no belief system or participation on the part of the one in need of healing. Yet how important are these distinctions?

There is something in Western thinking that seems to require boxes and separations for part of its security. In my way, there is a coupling of energies in the act of healing. The body emanates certain electro-magnetic vibrations, their strength determined by the harmony of mind, body, soul, spirit. Through the law of attraction, one who has an elevated vibration will attract energies of a healing nature. Most of us have had experiences of being attracted to someone or something. We say such persons have a magnetic personality. As we grow in consciousness, we draw to us those of the spirit world of like vibrations. The world of nature seems to be more magnetic, the world of spirit more luminous. Once we begin to use our magnetic and subtle energies for healing, as in therapeutic touch and crystal healing, we become more sensitive to the energies of nature. Using my own electro-magnetic field in harmony with a quartz crystal, the energy is amplified and magnified and will promote healing.

When one is led to the path of healer, a self-healing begins to take place, leading us to eventually find our spiritual selves and, through this realization, find reunion with Source, becoming "One who walks the path of Power." When we find our spiritual selves, the world of spirit becomes accessible and a second coupling takes place. We begin to see with more than our eyes, feel with other than our hands. We become luminous in nature and are held together with light.

Our true language is thought, touch and song. Somewhere we began to believe in the illusion we call the physical, rational world and separated ourselves from each other and that of Spirit. Through language and the concept of race, we lost much of our luminosity and became bound to our bodies in life.

Yet, this luminous self still exists within us. When mind, body, soul, spirit are in harmony, all around will be affected by that person's energy. There have been many instances when students attending my workshops have reported healing taking place after or during the sessions. One might say my magnetic field interacted with theirs in a healing way, unbeknown to me.

Each seminar or workshop I give is opened with the smoking of cedar and an offering of cornmeal to invoke the power of the Four Directions, Mother Earth, Father Sky, to come to aid and guide the work. These spiritual forces will have a healing influence on the whole group as well as on the one who may have a specific problem.

My understanding is based in harmony and coupling. If healing spirits are near they will have their own effect without me. I see in effect myself as a catalyst or a doorway. The personal is completely removed.

The crystals that are used for healing have their own power and energy, and do their work by just being in the proximity of the one in need of healing. When held in the hands, they can be programmed to specific ills. They will magnify the intentions of the healer, and through their purity, combine the forces of nature and spirit to channel healing energies. Yet, the crystals will remove pain, elevate one's vibration, promote clarity, help one to be less emotionally reactive, refract disharmonious energies, release negative ions, collect positive ions, and work with one's dreams, without any help from the two-legged. They have memory and attract the spirits of light. Yes, even the rocks shall sing the song of creation, even they shall reflect great mysteries of light . . .

Are these gifts mutually exclusive or can the Healer use any method at will?

We too often become more attached to method than to the actual healing. Many years ago, I asked Dr. Karl Menninger if he had one lesson to give me to guide the rest of my life, what would it be. He very quickly answered, "If it works, do it, and do it Now." When we do "street time," we find many innovative and creative ways to help heal, not only people but situations as well. Most healers have several methods and will often use several ways until the problem is solved. However, some healers may have more understanding and power in one area than others.

Can anyone be a Healer? Is healing an inborn gift or one that a dedicated student can acquire?

Healing is innate within most of our natures. It is society that closes us off to inborn abilities. When we wish to enhance the world through healing, we must become dedicated students of light within and without. When we are involved in an act of healing, we must be responsible to the one who is in need. Therefore, we should not romanticize or be egotistic or attached to the doing. We serve, and that is all we do. We serve as a channel, a vessel, emptied, surrendered, to be filled by power beyond our own understanding. We can work to enhance that which is inborn. Some perhaps have more innate abilities than others, yet it means nothing if it is not used and refined.

There are instances where healing powers have suddenly appeared later in life, often to one who had had no exposure to healing or spiritual ways. My great-grandmother once told me that talent, like singing, was a reflection of one who had been close to Source, the gift being given to remind people of the beauty of the Creator. It does not belong to the singer, and will be taken away if it is not used for the good of the people.

Many are born to walk the path of healing. My spirit was invoked to form in ceremony and born into a nine-sided star, drawn in crystals, because my great-grandmother and father conspired to set me firmly on this path. My feet were washed in the great waters of both oceans before my third birthday; my name designed to tie me to the power and need of Mother Earth.

What qualities are needed to become a channel for healing?

Anyone who wishes to help "make better" must develop a deep sense of love and compassion, which is a reflection of one's spiritual self in union with nature and Source. One must be willing to explore his own illnesses and loneliness and welcome change. Through the looking within, we may become truly empty, leaving space to be filled by That which is Above. We attach to and personalize our illnesses, claiming them as our own—my migraine, my cancer, my broken life. It seems the two-legged has a propensity for suffering. We cling to our psychosis and disease. If we give over our pain, what then will take its place?

We must practice surrender in our every moment, in our everyday lives. If we develop the quality of balance and emptiness, we will be working in harmony with the forces of nature and spirit all the time, therefore having a stronger effect for good in the world.

When my hair is braided for the ceremony used to open sharings with my students, my hands move in rhythm to a chant that centers me and helps the ego-self move aside. The left and right hemispheres of my brain become silent. Then Spirit may use my body, my voice. My feeling is one of openness, willingness, and a working together between the world of the physical and the world of Spirit. This is not to say that my being is subject to use by forces that are non-harmonious to my way.

What disciplines would you recommend?

The use of meditation and prayer to keep one in touch with humility, the study of philosophy, chemistry, nature, all of these will help.

A great deal of discipline is necessary for channeling healing energies in a conscious way. Learning to center through control of breath, sustaining optimum health on the physical and mental planes, thinking good thoughts require constant attention in this time of excesses and self-indulgences. My great-grandmother had me spend years just sitting with the plants, learning to commune with them before letting me cut and gather. She trained my mind to work on many levels, to register things and events beyond my ordinary senses.

Is it necessary to make a diagnosis? If so, how is it done?

A diagnosis would be helpful in most cases but not necessarily essential. My belief is that the physical symptom is the last to manifest. One must look to the disharmony of mind, body, soul and spirit and treat the cause. Perhaps the illness is the reflection of a past life. Let me give an example. Some years ago, a doctor friend sent me a patient who had suffered from bleeding ulcers for thirty of his thirty-seven years. Half of his stomach had been removed. A second surgery was suggested to replace the remaining stomach with one of plastic. During a healing ceremony performed for him, I drew energy down over his stomach. He began to scream: "The pain, the pain!" He then began to cry and spoke of what he saw—a man (himself) running, being pursued, shot in the stomach, left to bleed to death in the snow.

He still has his half a stomach, and is free of ulcers. No matter if it is an actual remembrance of past life; somehow he freed his blocked energies and was healed.

Does unusual heat emanate from the hands of the healer?

For myself, this has been the usual experience, the patient also feeling heat and a sense of well-being. There have been times in my life when the sudden rise of heat in my hands indicated my being in the presence of one who was ill. Upon further examination, the person indeed had some illness of a serious nature. Our bodies are capable of receiving information much faster than our rational, thinking minds. When we experience changes in our physiology such as sudden temperature drop, clammy hands, heart acceleration or sudden heat, we should pay particular attention to the people and events around us. *Is a healer tired or refreshed after a treatment?*

A feeling of well being and energy are usually felt. Those who feel depleted perhaps are not processing the energy properly. We can become attached even to the pain of others.

The medical school of the "survival of the fittest" does not incorporate methods for the processing of subtle energies. Perhaps this is why the number one disease of doctors is hypertension. One may become easily depleted if attached as a doer. Healing energies should flow through one as easily as breath, as clear as the light after a morning rain.

Does the healer consciously raise his vibration and generate psychic energy?

Many techniques are used to raise vibrations, such as chanting, singing, dance, meditation. Sometimes the elevation takes place in spite of our resistance. We are not always conscious of the process, though we should be able to exercise more control. The way of thinking in the West is to believe us to be omnipotent to the point of trying to control the forces of nature. Yet in one volcanic eruption, the earth is changed and the skies are filled with ash. We should not try to manipulate nature but rather harmonize with the forces of all living things. Through this harmony, our elevated vibration will utilize energies from above and below. We carry this spark of Infinite One. Somewhere in life's journey, the spark is flamed and we begin to expand outward in fire, burning off the solidity of our bitter resistance. We seek the light without, once having seen light within ourselves. We become aware of innate psychic abilities and, through care and discipline, we finally pass through the door that takes us to this Infinite One where we find the Source of all power. We walk the path to Conscious Perfect Being.

We are ultimately responsible for our own consciousness. We should, indeed, approach the Infinite with humility.

Does the healer connect with a healing guide? A pool of cosmic wisdom? Or achieve oneness through prayer?

This question is partially answered in the previous one. It is indeed all three but not always at the same time.

As a small child about three years old, my stubborn self disobeyed and went to the sandbox in spite of warnings about the wind, which caught tin roofing and sent it crashing down upon the top of my head, fracturing my skull. My experience was a sudden seeing—a very tall Indian man who said, "My name is Mithra. Do not be afraid. You are not alone." After a month when I was in and out of consciousness and not getting any better, my father finally heard of this tall man who came every dawn and every sunset and held his hand above my fevered head. He sent for my great-grandmother who asked me to tell her from which direction the tall man came. She faced that direction and spoke to the space, filling it with her vibrations, magnified through the crystals she held in her hand. She later told my father that the spirit said there was something inside the skull that must be removed immediately. It was quite an experience for my father and great-grandmother to convince the doctor to reopen and examine the wound on the basis of her conversation with space and a child's supposed delirium. The equivalent of four teaspoons of hair was removed from the interior of my skull.

This man walked by my side until I was nine years old. To me, it has always been natural to call upon the spirits for various reasons. No one ever told me it was special or different.

The pool of cosmic wisdom is reached through this journey to consciousness. It includes knowledge tested in the laboratory of our life's experiences. It is reached through an act of surrender where one becomes empty enough to be filled again with light. My belief is that truth is vibratory. We feel the truth when we hear it, read it, see it, sing it. We feel it everywhere. We find it everywhere. Glimmers of it are in everyone's way.

In vision, my life was given over to the path of light, expressed through service to the great goddess of the universes, mother of all living things. It is now possible for me to handle a book, flip through its pages and have a knowing of its contents. This is a dip into the pool of cosmic wisdom. Once we touch the truth, we know how vast creation really is and how small, yet important a part of the whole we are. It brings one a measure of humility, and prayer becomes as common as breath. Life becomes the prayer. Through prayer we may lose some of our arrogance and resistance and finally come to realize we bathe in the pool of cosmic wisdom through communication with Source. We then live to be a reflection of the great knowing.

Does the healing process differ for different problems such as mental illness, deformities, viruses, arthritis, cancer, etc.?

Healing processes do differ for various problems and reasons. However, it is most difficult for me to separate healing into taking care of various conditions. There must be harmony of mind, body, soul, spirit, or the physical will begin to deteriorate. For example, when a child is seriously ill, we treat the entire family, believing the most sensitive and vulnerable reflect the whole. Each healing is designed for the total problem, including the mind, body, soul and spirit of all involved.

Are there any limitations on the healing process?

To answer this question, I must examine concepts somewhat foreign to me. We are so attached to our lives, we believe the only way to heal is for the body to survive. Crossing from life to life to life is a healing. In each life we become more conscious, shed more of the effects of our past life's causes, grow to illumination which will eventually lead to freedom, to be free of doom. Doom is only such when one believes death is not an act of consciousness. Sometimes the choice is to go forward to heal in the Presence. When we see that one has made the choice to go from this world of illusion to the world of spirit, we should begin the preparation for the ultimate experience of life so one might cross over in consciousness, free of the fear of death.

Why are all people not healed at a healing session?

My feelings are mixed in regard to this question. In my way, one is very careful and certain of anyone who will be involved in a healing, making sure anyone present is in harmony with the event, casting no questionable vibrations on the healing. For groups who gather to heal, even those whose bodies are not healed have experienced healing on some level. The skeptic who came to scoff will be affected by the healing vibrations, for after all the true transforming power is love, and any who are near its expression will be made better on some level. The Western world is so quick to judge the effect of the healing without considering the long-term results. Because of a standard description of what a healing constitutes, they miss many little miracles as they look for the magnificent, obvious ones.

Is the healing treatment to be given only once to a patient, or must it be renewed?

Treatment is always based on the individual need. When working with one on physical levels, sometimes one session is all that is needed, or sometimes several treatments are indicated, dependent on how attached one is to the diseases and problems. There have been occasions where treatment at a distance will have beneficial results after one session. Often in faith healing especially, healing takes place immediately.

Will the healing process continue if the healer stops treatment?

The healing process will continue. However, my belief is that once we share this space of feeling with another, treatment never stops until the sick one is indeed made better.

Can reasons be given for the failure of a treatment?

It is almost impossible for me to associate healing with failure. Again, it is only a way of thinking in terms of judgment that says this is failure, this is success. Each will progress according to his or her own individual needs. Those needs are not always met by the body's clinging to this life.

Does the healer visualize the illness and then visualize it as cured, or does he visualize a perfect and healthy person from the start?

Visualizations play an important part of healing, even in the allopathic world of medicine. My learning always led me to first see the problem as it is; then to let it go, having been freed of its vibrations by recognizing, then discarding it; then to see the person whole, well, clinging to this visualization until the problem is solved.

Is the touch of the healer's hands necessary? What purpose does it serve?

We touch with our hands in many ways. When passing my hands through the fields* of one who needs to be made better without touching the physical body, my experience is of touching in a more subtle manner. When healing at a distance, my hands have no contact in the

---

*Subtle electro-magnetic emanations from a person's body.

physical. Energy is not limited by the confines of space and many times others are touched by healing energies though thousands of miles may separate us. Then again, hands may actually experience the illness and communicate to the mind of the healer what the problem is. Sometimes physical touch is indicated, for truly nothing communicates our love and desire to help quicker than a comforting caress or a deeply felt hug. We two-leggeds are very tactile creatures, life being the gift of touch.

Come, sweet life
Come give me, once again
the touch of
body, rock, sea.
Caress my being with
rain, wind, cold.
Let me know the guileless kiss
of a child,
or a lover's return.
Feel the cool, sweet cleansing
of tears gone
like wild rivers
running down the
valley of my face.
Come, sweet life,
fuse my spirit with the
means of
animating
my soul
to touch again.
Then—
all is made beautiful.

What is the role of the patient?

My response to the word *role* in this context is counter to my concept of what takes place in healing. The word *role* indicates that one is separate from the reality of life and must fill a role instead of just being who they are.

What are the reported sensations of the patients?

Responses to a healing vary dramatically according to the individual. Some may become very emotional and try to reject the healer. Almost everyone reports a relaxation response which will help alleviate tension, thereby promoting the beginning of self-healing.

Can the patient be benefited simply by his proximity to a healer without conscious volition on the part of the healer?

Some years ago, it was my privilege to accompany my grandfather, David Monongye, who is one of the Hopi elders and spiritual leaders, to the United Nations Conference on Ecology in Stockholm, Sweden. There was a Third World alternate conference in progress simultaneously with that of the United Nations. Grandfather was the last on a panel of speakers. By the time the 'talking stick reached him, everyone in the room was angry and they were all convinced that their needs were greater than any others. The intensity of the vibrations was almost overwhelming. Grandfather stood quietly. When his turn came, he stood, head bowed in prayer over a bit of corn meal offering in his hand. He prayed in silence, a language we all understand. He prayed until every voice was quiet, every person stilled. He told the world that we are all brothers and sisters in Great Spirit's creation and, by the act of loving, we might begin to truly know and help each other. A tremendous healing took place then. To this day it vibrates through the far reaches of our planet. The yearly Earthday celebrations are the result of that moment's healing. Many came to me later and spoke of how the hardness and bitterness had left their hearts. This is only one level of how healing may manifest without conscious volition. However, somewhere deep within us, we know through our intuitive natures, when we are needed or called upon.

One of my dear friends and apprentices was ready to deliver her first child. She could not find me in the physical anywhere, and this was to be my godchild. Remembering my words to her of not becoming too dependent on physical contact for communication, she took a crystal I had given her for that purpose and called to me. That night, she dreamed my presence took her in a cave and taught her how to birth in a spiritual manner, so the child's life would be blessed in both the natural and spiritual worlds. When we spoke of it, I knew she had received all of the ceremony in the dream. She even remembered such an elusive concept as tying a blue heron or eagle feather loosely in a tree overnight, that if it is there at dawn, the spirits of wind and night have kissed it, stars have infused it with light, Grandmother Moon has blessed it with her shining.

How can we know the many instances in which we cross the confines of time and space because we are tuned to the needs of another.

Can a patient at a distance and unaware of the healer's efforts on his behalf be healed?

There are ways of doing healing at a distance that do not require the cooperation of the one who is out of harmony. However, the awareness of the one in need of healing is most helpful, especially when there is a life-threatening situation. In a crystal healing ceremony a picture or drawing of the person or event or even the name written on a piece of paper is all that is needed.

Can unconscious people, babies and animals, be healed by the efforts of the healer?

In a medical sense, a person is considered unconscious if his eyes are unfocused, with no visible responses, and he is unable to communicate. *We* believe one is unconscious when living in selfish and greedy ways.

During the Indian occupation of the penal island of Alcatraz some years ago, one Mohawk leader, Richard Oakes, was struck down with a severly fractured skull. He lay in a state of unconsciousness nearly a month. Across the room from him, in the San Francisco General Hospital I.C.U., was another man who suffered similar injuries in a trucking accident. He was not from California and knew nothing of the occupation of the islands. Yet often, I myself, and others heard this man speak of Alcatraz, Richard's wife, Mad Bear, a Tuscorora medicine man, and other things pertaining to the Indian struggle. Richard was never left alone. We touched him, made gifts for him, and waited for the hospital authorities to give permission for Richard to be doctored Indian way. When he finally reached critical crisis and was pronounced clinically dead, the Medicine Men were allowed to do what they had waited a month in the hall for. Richard lived. They said he would never walk or talk again. He did both.

We know so very little of worlds beyond the physical. My own personal experience while in a coma was frequently seeing the events around me from outside my body.

Children are extremely receptive to magnetic and spiritual healing. They have not attached themselves to illnesses and their minds are still free and receptive enough to respond. Babies are like wondrous little sponges and their fields will absorb healing energies quickly, for there is no resistance to shield them from its influences. Because of this sensitivity, one should be very gentle in dealing with infants and little people. The same is true of animals.

Can a scoffer be healed in spite of his refusal to take the healing effort seriously?

Some years back twenty skeptical, agnostic or atheist, hostile physicians were involved in an experiment with me in which crystals, earth, trees, and visualizations were all that were used as a prescription to alleviate their suffering from hypertension. Within a year, seventeen of the twenty were free of all symptomatology and medication.

My feeling is that the scoffer will force us to validate our personal experiences in healing, in tune with the other more understood sciences, and refine our methods and information so that they are replicable.

What is the most cooperative and ideal behavior on the part of the patient?

There is no ideal behavior. When one is ill, the ideal is to be well again, to be free of both cause and effect. A cooperative patient merely accepts whatever energies the healing is dealing with. Sometimes resistance to disease holds one from healing, the same as attachment can.

What is the healing process?

The earth is our Mother. Everything in our life in the form of material support comes from the Mother Earth. Even the money spent for food is made from her trees whose roots reach deep into her soil. She is a living, breathing organism, has nerve and heart, even as myself. We cannot live without our hearts. This is true even when our hearts are broken romantically. So, often the result is an attempted suicide or consideration of such, for we cannot live without our hearts.

The land of the southwestern four corners is called the heart of the Mother Earth, bound by four breathing mountains, protected by rock crystal girl and rock crystal boy, Mount Blanca in Colorado, Mount Taylor in New Mexico, Mount Hesperice in Utah, San Francisco peaks in

Arizona, connected by a ley line to the sacred Black Hills of the Dakotas. We are told in prophecy these lands should remain undisturbed until after purification is completed. As usual, the government encourages big business to go for the resources without regard to the reasons the native peoples hold these lands so sacred. My thought is that perhaps the heart of Mother Earth is the western electro-magnetic pole. Perhaps that is why this region has the highest incidence of lightning phenomena in the world and strata filled with quartz crystals which attract lightning. What of the discharge of positive ions here? We know so little. Dare we not listen to a people like the Hopis who have a phenomenally high incidence of accuracy in prophecy?

We cannot live without our life support system which is our Mother Earth. How very unintelligent of us to allow others to destroy the very things that sustain our existence. What of the unborn and their right to life as the gift of touch? There can be no true healing until we stop the wounding and heal Mother Earth. The two-legged is the endangered species, and all others reflect our own endangerment. We can help heal conditions in mind, body, soul and spirit in individuals, but it is meaningless if we let the earth die.

We are very grateful to the five healers who have enlightened these pages, and we end with the Sufi greeting to them, *Ya Azim*, which means, "How beautifully you manifest the divine glory to me."

Nancy and Esmond Gardner

QUEST BOOKS
are published by
The Theosophical Society in America
a branch of a world organization
dedicated to the promotion of brotherhood and
the encouragement of the study of religion,
philosophy, and science, to the end that man may
better understand himself and his place in
the universe. The Society stands for complete
freedom of individual search and belief.
In the Theosophical Classics Series
well-known occult works are made
available in popular editions.